Econometric Models Of the Housing Sector

A POLICY-ORIENTED SURVEY

J. ERIC FREDLAND
C. DUNCAN MACRAE

The Urban Institute is a nonprofit research corporation established in 1968 to study problems of the nation's urban communities. Independent and nonpartisan, the Institute responds to current needs for disinterested analyses and basic information and attempts to facilitate the application of this knowledge. As part of this effort, it cooperates with federal agencies, states, cities, associations of public officials, the academic community and other sectors of the general public.

The Institute's research findings and a broad range of interpretive viewpoints are published as an educational service. Conclusions expressed in Institute publications are those of the authors and do not necessarily reflect the views of other staff members, officers or trustees of the Institute, or of organizations which provide funds toward support of Institute studies.

These research findings are made available in three series of publications: Books and Reports, Papers, and Reprints. A current publications list is available on request.

Publications Office

The Urban Institute
2100 M Street, N.W.
Washington, D.C. 20037

Econometric Models Of the Housing Sector

A POLICY-ORIENTED SURVEY

J. ERIC FREDLAND
C. DUNCAN MACRAE

250-1-1

August 1978

THE URBAN INSTITUTE
WASHINGTON, D.C.

The research forming the basis for this publication was funded by the Office of Policy Development and Research, U.S. Department of Housing and Urban Development, through Contract H-2162R.

The interpretations or conclusions are those of the authors and should not be attributed to The Urban Institute, its trustees, or to other organizations that support its research.

ISBN 87766-232-0

UI 250-1-1

PLEASE REFER TO URI 23600 WHEN ORDERING

Available from:

Publications Office
The Urban Institute
2100 M Street, N.W.
Washington, D.C. 20037

List price: $5.00

A/78/1M

TABLE OF CONTENTS

FOREWORD

This paper is one of a series of special housing analyses funded in FY 1977 by the Institute's Housing Group under Contract H-2162R (Task Order 31). The overall objective of the Task Order was to assist the Office of Policy Development and Research, U.S. Department of Housing and Urban Development, in its long-range research planning activities by contributing concrete, specific ideas for housing research based on a larger framework of emerging policy-related problems and issues. These analyses were intended to lead to both action-oriented demonstrations and studies, and, where necessary, to more basic investigations to gain a better understanding of the underlying phenomena upon which to base policy and programs. Wyndham Clarke was the Government Technical Representative for this task.

Morton Isler
Director of Housing Studies

ACKNOWLEDGMENT

This research was supported by funds from the Office of Policy Development and Research, U.S. Department of Housing and Urban Development, under Contract No. H-2162R to The Urban Institute. Opinions expressed are those of the authors and do not necessarily represent the views of the Department of Housing and Urban Development, The Urban Institute, or its sponsors.

We wish to thank Robert Buckley, James Follain, Morton Isler, and Richard Muth for many helpful comments and Echo Innes for careful typing of the manuscript.

INTRODUCTION

During the past 20 years, a number of econometric models have been developed to explain the level and character of activity in residential construction at the national level. This expanding literature was last surveyed comprehensively by Grebler and Maisel in 1963 (A5), although there have been several surveys since then directed at a portion of the literature (see particularly Fair (A2); Fromm (A3); Edwards (A1); and Kearl, Rosen, and Swan (A7), (A7a)). The purpose of this paper is to provide a comprehensive survey of U.S. literature from 1960 through 1977, with particular emphasis on the use of models for addressing issues of public policy.

The models considered here all attempt to explain housing starts (number or value) or investment in residential construction. Included are models of the housing sector per se, for example the Maisel model (C10) and the Huang model (C5), and the housing equations of national models such as the Bureau of Economic Analysis (BEA) model (B4), the MIT-Pennsylvania-SSRC (MPS) model (B13), and the Wharton Mark IV model (B18). Models developed primarily to analyze financial markets, for example the Bosworth-Duesenberry model (B2), are not excluded if they contain starts or investment equations.

The literature search has been approached by examining the Journal of Economic Literature (categories 315-Credit; 634-Construction; 932-Housing), survey articles of various aspects of the field, bibliographies of works reviewed, Federal Home Loan Bank Board working papers, and other sources. No systematic attempt has been made to collect unpublished materials, although unpublished sources were examined, particularly relating to some of the national models on which published material is sparse. Unpublished sources are listed in the bibliography if the materials are generally available. The bibliography contains references to papers which directly discuss the housing models or housing sectors, papers which contain the housing equations of national models, even if the housing sector is not the focus of the paper itself, data sources, and selected works which are often cited by, or discuss issues raised in, the model literature.

The remainder of the paper contains five major sections in addition to the bibliography. Model specification can be viewed as a function of the underlying theory and available data. Accordingly, in Section I, the basic theory of the housing sector is described, and housing data is the subject of Section II. Section III presents a brief discussion of estimation methods employed. In Section IV, empirical results of policy analyses performed with the models are discussed. Section V contains some conclusions regarding the use of the models surveyed in policy analysis. Throughout the paper, the models are extensively cross-referenced, and an index is provided for the convenience of a reader interested in a particular model.

The paper is written for economists and others who are not primarily experts in the housing field. The experts will find that much of the material presented here is familiar, although to them the paper should be a useful reference document.

I. HOUSING THEORY

In this section, the theory of the housing sector is described. We view the housing sector as consisting of four interdependent markets: housing services, real estate production, construction inputs, and mortgage credit. After an overview, each of the four markets is discussed in turn. Then the interactions among the markets are examined. Finally, policies are categorized in terms of the market in which they have their direct impact.

Overview

The housing sector can be viewed as consisting of four markets. These are markets for: (1) the flow of housing services from the available stock of housing; (2) the flow of residential construction--or, more correctly, real estate production, including both structure and land--which adds to the available stock; (3) the flow of mortgage credit; and (4) the flow of construction inputs. While the focus here is on the residential construction market, it is impossible to discuss models of the housing sector without considering the other three, particularly since the centerpiece of many residential construction models is not that market, but one of the others, usually the mortgage market. Accordingly, we will describe the characteristics of each, but keep the discussion of all but the second (residential construction) relatively rudimentary.

One may view the four markets as being related schematically:

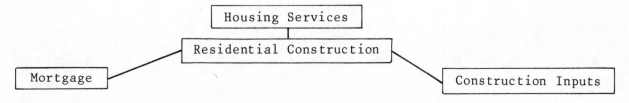

The market for housing services together with the mortgage market underlie the demand side of the residential construction market. Underlying the supply side is the market for construction inputs. Supply and demand in each of the underlying markets in turn, of course, are functionally related to other markets, which also receive a certain amount of attention in the residential construction literature. For example, a number of papers focus on the determinants of the flow of funds into financial intermediaries, particularly savings and loan associations (S&Ls) and mutual savings banks (MSBs), which supply mortgage credit. See, for example, Sparks (C13) and Silber (B15). There is a large literature on housing services markets, but there is relatively little attention within it to residential construction. See deLeeuw (F10), Paldam (F36), and Polinsky (F37) for surveys of some of this literature.

While we will describe each component as a single market, it is important to note that each is in fact a network of geographically distinct markets. The appropriate level of disaggregation differs among the four. The relevant market for housing services is metropolitan or neighborhood in character. The real estate production market is metropolitan for single-family construction, metropolitan or regional for most multifamily construction, and national for mobile homes. The construction input markets are metropolitan, regional, or national depending on the particular input being considered. Land markets are neighborhood and metropolitan; labor markets are metropolitan or regional, at least in the short run; many materials markets are national. Mortgage markets are regional or national.

Little geographical disaggregation has been attempted in the literature surveyed, despite the theoretical correctness of such disaggregation. Lack of suitable data has been a particular barrier. A few papers have addressed this problem. Fair (D1) applied his national model to SMSA data for 14 SMSAs, using building permits as the dependent variable. Results were partially or wholly acceptable in terms of expected signs in only eight of 14 cases. Krekorian (D4) models the residential construction sector of Pomona, California. Winger, in a series of papers (D8, D10, D11), examines regional markets and concludes that interregional migration has important impacts on residential construction regionally. Bebee (E1) produced a regional Canadian model.

Every model of the residential construction sector deals with these four component "blocks" in one way or another. The models vary widely in degree of detail and sophistication, of course. A few provide a relatively complete specification in terms of the theory presented below--particularly the MPS (B13) and BEA (B4) models--but most do not. Many of the models involve a single equation representation of the entire sector, or a series of single equation estimates using somewhat different specifications, or disaggregating the dependent variable. Examples include Maisel (C10a), Burnham (C10c), Swan (C14), Brady (C2), Muth (C11), and VonFurstenberg-Herr (C17). The equation may be interpreted as a reduced form explaining starts in some cases, or as a supply or a demand equation in others, although, as Fair points out (A2), in some cases the equations cannot really be interpreted as any of these. Several models estimate separate supply and demand equations for residential construction or a demand equation for housing services and a supply equation for construction. Among the housing sector models, examples include Arcelus-Meltzer (C1), Huang (C5), Rosen-Kearl (C12), and Swan (C15). National models typically offer complex multiequation specifications of the housing sector but do not estimate separate supply and demand equations. BEA (B4), Brookings (B3), Chase (B5), DRI (B7), and Wharton Mark IV (B18) are among those that fit into this category. Fair (B8) estimates supply and demand for starts. MPS (B13) estimates demand for supply and demand for starts.

Housing Services Market

As we noted above, the market for housing services is at most metropolitan in character. Indeed, neighborhood characteristics are important. Not only is the stock of real estate immobile, but people are not fully mobile within metropolitan areas, much less between them. Thus, the market is really a highly segmented composite of neighborhood markets. The markets within an area are highly interactive--see Muth (F35) and deLeeuw and Struyk (F12) for detailed discussion of the metropolitan housing market. In short, there is no national market for housing services, but rather a series of metropolitan and submetropolitan markets. This is important to note, although very little of the literature with which we are concerned disaggregates geographically, because there are significant variations in residential construction between and within metropolitan areas.

In accord with the standard theory of consumer behavior, we can describe the demand for units of flow of housing services, where a unit of flow of housing services is theoretically standardized for quality and space:

$$D_h = f(R_{RE}, P_o, Y, DEM, W).$$

Demand (D_h) is represented as a function of the price, or rental rate, per unit of housing services (R_{RE}), prices of other goods and services (P_o), income (Y), wealth (W), and tastes (DEM). Tastes in this context are in large measure--although not exclusively--a matter of demographics. Population size, family size, population age structure, and marriage rates are among demographic factors influencing the demand for housing services. The appropriate price of housing variable includes both explicit rental rates and implicit rental rates on owner-occupied housing. Given the durable nature of housing, permanent income is the theoretically correct income concept.

Whether or not they separate theoretically or statistically the market for housing services from the market for residential construction, all models make use of some of these demand variables. Many, but not all, include the price variables. Among those that do not are DRI (B7) and, as estimated, the Brady models (C2), (C3). Several models use a permanent income proxy (for example, MPS (B13), BEA (B4), Rosen and Kearl (C12), and Huang (C5)); others use some measure of current income (for example, Chase (B5) and Wharton Annual (B17)); and many contain no income variable at all (for example, Maisel (C10a), Fair (B8), and VonFurstenberg-Herr (C17)). Most models do not contain explicit wealth measures (but see DRI (B7) and Arcelus-Meltzer (C1)). Demographic factors are not commonly considered in short-run models. These so called "basic demand factors" are not subject to sharp short-run shifts and their occasional presence in quarterly models (for example, see Maisel (C10a), Rosen and Kearl (C12), and Brookings (B3)) adds little explanatory power. However, the long-cycle literature, discussed briefly below, concentrates much attention on demographics.

The short-run supply of housing services can be represented as

$$S_h = f(KH, P_m),$$

where KH is the stock of real estate (structures plus land), and P_m is the price of operating inputs, i.e., consumer durables and periodic maintenance. Three to five years durability is usually assumed to distinguish operating inputs from additions to real estate. Most models assume, at least implicitly, that the flow of housing services is directly proportional to the stock of real estate, and that there is little substitutibility between real estate additions and operating inputs. Further, since the flow of residential construction in a given year is small relative to the size of the stock, the supply of services is viewed as perfectly inelastic with respect to price in the short run. See Kalchbrenner (B13d) for an explicit statement of this supply relationship. In the very long run, the supply of housing services, while still proportional to the stock, reflects supply conditions in residential construction. The long-run supply is quite elastic, as is discussed below. In the intermediate period, which in the housing sector is a matter of a number of years, the supply of housing services should reflect both the inelastic character of the existing stock and the elastic nature of the supply of residential construction. Nearly all of the models considered here are short-run models.

The rental price per standard unit of housing services is determined by the interaction of supply and demand in each market. Within a metropolitan area, of course, there is a spectrum of rental rates differing according to accessibility and the existence of externalities. At any particular time, the rental price is not likely to be at a market clearing level. Both excess demand and excess supply situations will exist in different metropolitan-neighborhood markets, and one or the other may dominate in the aggregate. Disequilibrium is reflected in part by levels of vacancies. The role of vacancies is complex. There are two types: available units and nonavailable units. Nonavailable vacancies include vacation and second dwellings, units sold or rented but not yet occupied, and dilapidated units removed from the housing stock. It is available vacancies that play a role in the market adjustment process. Excess supply in the housing services market is indicated by the existence of numerous unoccupied available units; excess demand by the lack of such units. Market equilibrium is characterized by some vacancy rate greater than zero. A housing services market is characterized by a search process in which both buyers and sellers are seeking matches. Given a volume of moves (turnover) and the heterogeneity of the housing stock in any market, there is an economically efficient level of vacancies reflecting the search process. An increased number of moves, given the stock and no change in the flow of information, will yield a higher equilibrium vacancy rate; an area with a relatively homogeneous stock will, given a volume of moves, have a relatively low equilibrium vacancy rate. The vacancy rate will deviate from its equilibrium level when the rental rate per unit of housing services adjusts incompletely to a change in demand for--or supply of--housing services. The short-run excess demand (supply) is absorbed by decreases (increases) in vacancy rates. As will be noted below, the supply of residential construction responds both to changes in the prices of housing services and to changes in vacancy rates. The work of Maisel particularly emphasizes the role of vacancies (see particularly C10a and B3a) and various models contain vacancy equations (for example, DRI (B7) and Wharton Mark IV (B18)) or vacancy variables (for example, Swan (C15a), (C15b), Bosworth-Duesenberry (B2a), and Rosen and Kearl (C12)). Many models, however (for example, MPS (B13), Arcelus-Meltzer (C1), and Michigan (B14)), do not consider vacancies.

Real Estate Production Market

Overview

The link between the housing services market and the real estate production market lies in basic capital theory. First, consider a simple capital stock adjustment equation:

$$RC = \alpha(K^* - K_a) + \beta K_a,$$

where RC is the flow of residential construction, defined in terms of standard units, adjusted for quality and space; K^* is the desired stock of real estate; and K_a is the existing stock of real estate. If the flow of housing services is proportional to the stock of real estate, the demand for those services can be viewed as reflecting the desired stock of real estate, K^*. The existing stock delivers a proportional flow of services. A gap between the desired stock and the actual stock where $K^* > K_a$ induces investment in residential construction. If $K^* < K_a$, the rate of production is depressed. The final term on the right hand side represents replacement investment to maintain the stock.

The inducement to invest lies not in the gap per se, of course, but in the effect of the gap on the relative profitability of investment in residential construction. The gross rate of return on real estate, defined as the rental rate on real estate (R_{RE}) divided by the cost price of real estate (P_k), for the marginal investment in competitive equilibrium, will cover the cost of capital as reflected by the appropriate interest rate, in this case the mortgage rate (i), plus physical depreciation of structure (μ), plus property taxes (τ), less expected capital gains $\left(\dfrac{\dot{P}_{RE}}{P_{RE}}\right)$

$$\frac{R_{RE}}{P_k} = i + \mu + \tau - \frac{\dot{P}_{RE}}{P_{RE}}$$

Each term should be adjusted for income taxes as appropriate. An increase in the demand for housing services, opening a gap between the desired and actual stock above, induces increases in rental prices of housing services (R_{RE}), which, by pushing up the rate of return on real estate relative to the cost of capital, induces investment. The increase in demand for housing services will also drive down vacancy rates, which does not affect the rate of return directly, but does affect anticipations concerning future rates of return.

Equivalently, we can view the asset price of real estate (P_{RE}) as equal to the discounted present value of the rental stream:

$$P_{RE} = \frac{R_{RE}}{i}$$

with terms defined as before. Note the assumption here is that the return is received in perpetuity, which is not unreasonable for structures, given their durability, but is not reasonable for mobile homes. Adjusted for expected capital gains, depreciation, and property taxes, the equation becomes:

$$P_{RE} = \frac{R_{RE} + \dot{P}_{RE}}{i + \mu + \tau}$$

Viewed in this light, the asset price per unit of real estate, P_{RE}, is a bid price, which in competitive equilibrium is equal to the cost price, P_k. Changes in the demand for housing services cause the rental rate and thus the asset price to change. The relationship between the bid price and the cost price is thus affected, which in turn affects the investment decision. Many models, beginning with Muth's pioneering work in 1960 (C11), are grounded in a basic capital stock adjustment equation. Examples include Wharton Mark IV (B18), DRI (B7), and VonFurstenberg-Herr (C17). The MPS (B13) and BEA (B4) models are explicitly cast in the capital asset pricing framework described above. Other models are not.

Demand

The demand for real estate production is, then, derived from the market for housing services and the cost of capital, which is determined in the mortgage market, and is reflected in the bid price for real estate, (P_{RE}). It should be noted that real estate production includes not merely starts, but also additions and alterations, as distinct from maintenance, to the existing stock. Given a single rental rate for real estate, and a single mortgage rate, the bid price in essence represents a horizontal demand curve for residential construction. In fact, there is a spectrum of bid prices within a metropolitan area. The demand curve has the traditional slope because rental rates differ depending on accessibility and external effects and because effective interest rates differ with class of tenant. Low-income tenants are thought to be higher risks. Effective interest rates also vary because of variations in effective tax rates. Note that we are speaking of units standardized for space and quality, so rental rates do not differ because units are nonstandard.

The market demand curve for real estate production in a metropolitan area is, then, the summation of demand in all neighborhoods. Given a high cost price, there are few neighborhoods in which the discounted value of the rental stream (P_{RE}) exceeds the cost price (P_k). As the cost price falls or as the demand for housing services rises, more neighborhoods are drawn into the market. Given a constant rental rate, variations in effective interest rates will tend to put high-income people "near the top" of the demand curve. When production of real estate is relatively small, it is for wealthier people because their lower effective interest rate induces them to bid higher prices for new real estate units. Less wealthy individuals are priced out of the market. Of course, low-income individuals may be prevented from bidding by some sort of capital rationing as well. Variations in rental rates may wash out the effect of differential interest costs. It may be that rental rates are high for low-income individuals, or that there is significant market segmentation, accompanied by excess supply in the high-income market.

Supply

The supply of new real estate is a function of the prices of inputs--labor, capital, materials, land--which aggregate to a cost price (or spectrum of cost prices), the bid price of real estate, and builders' expectations of future prices of real estate. In many models, it is assumed that the costs of inputs are fixed and that they are readily available--in effect, that the supply curve of residential construction is perfectly elastic. For some econometric evidence of this supply curve, see Muth (C11), Kartman (D3), and Cassidy-Valentini (C4). Pollock (D5), using cross section data, finds that supply is relatively inelastic. One model (MPS) has at one time included a capacity constraint, but the variable has had little significance (Kalchbrenner (B13c), pp. 114-115). If the supply curve is horizontal, the gap between the bid price(s) and the cost price, plus builder-investor expectations regarding that gap, determine the amount of construction in any period--construction is demand determined, subject perhaps to financing constraints (see Fair (B8) and Swan (C15) for models built explicitly along the latter line).

It is important to disaggregate the supply side by type of residential construction because technology and input mix differ considerably among them. There are four main types: single-family structures, multifamily structures, mobile homes, renovations and additions. Single-family production is land intensive; multifamily, relatively capital and skilled labor intensive; mobile homes are a product of the manufacturing sector, not the construction industry, and their production is capital and transportation intensive. The need to disaggregate stems from two considerations--first, it is not clear that inputs are particularly mobile across sectors, and the short-run supply curve for a particular type of construction may not be perfectly elastic. Thus, the mix of types of starts changes with variations in the strength of demand. Second, production periods differ markedly across type. Particularly, the production period for multifamily units is considerably longer on average than that for single-family units. (See Cassidy (Gc)4) for an estimate of the time profile of production.) These lags affect the rate at which the "demand gap" is filled, since it is completed units, not starts, that actually deliver housing services. Further, and of considerable practical importance, if the output of a model is investment in residential construction and not starts, the mix of production must be considered, since the amount of investment in any period depends on starts over several periods --the number depending on the production period and thus on the type of construction.

Not surprisingly, since their output is investment in residential construction, the larger national models do disaggregate by type of structure, usually with separate equations for the single-family and for the multifamily sector. (For example, see MPS, Wharton Mark IV, Wharton Annual, and Chase.) The current version of the BEA model separates one to four units and five or more, and one version of Brookings provides equations for one, two, and three or more units (B3d). The DRI model (B7b) has a single equation for starts, but separates one to four units and five or more units in the residential construction equation.

In contrast, the majority of models of the housing sector alone makes no distinction among types of starts. Exceptions include Huang (C5), who estimates supply and demand equations for single- and multifamily units, and Brady (C3). Several models consider only one type of start—for example, Huang (D2) and McDonough (C9) consider only single-family; Taubman and Rasche (D7), only multifamily.

Few models deal explicitly with mobile homes despite their recent importance, due in large part to lack of suitable data. Data are now being collected and most future models will doubtless include mobile homes equations. Among those containing a mobile homes equation are DRI (B7), Chase (B5), and Brady (C3).

In models of the housing sector alone, in which output is starts, additions and alterations can be ignored. In models in which residential construction is estimated, this type of construction must be included in some way, explicitly or implicitly. It is explicit and exogenous in BEA (B4), assumed proportional to the stock in Brookings and MPS. The Chase model, however, contains a behavioral equation explaining additions and alterations. As we have noted, builder expectations, as well as input and bid prices, affect construction in a given period of time; modeling expectation ultimately involves deciding what information builders use in assessing future profit prospects. Among possible factors are: recent behavior of sales; recent behavior of vacancy rates; the trends in rental prices; the state of the mortgage market, as measured by mortgage rates and perhaps by the availability of funds; the "state of the economy"; and—in the longer run—interregional migration and other demographic trends. Expectations will, of course, differ across regional markets. They will also differ by type of construction. Single-family structures are built (1) by owners themselves, (2) to order, by builders, (3) to stock by builder-developers. Expectational factors play a relatively small role in the first two cases, but are important in the third. Multifamily builder-developers typically seek investors and build for them. Expectations on the part of the investors are key to the investment decision. Expectations regarding long-run factors are more important here than for single-family construction. Mobile homes are produced to stock. Expectations are important, but regional differences are not significant. Most models contain variables in the starts or supply of starts equations which could be interpreted as expectational factors. Two papers which develop an inventory theoretic approach to single-family starts in which expectations are explicitly discussed are McDonough (C9) and Huang (D2). Huang concentrates only on speculative (builder initiated) starts as distinct from owner-initiated starts.

Market Equilibrium

The equilibrium price of real estate ($P_{RE} = P_k$) is determined by the interaction of supply and demand as described above. The basic model as described so far can be depicted as follows:

Housing Services Market

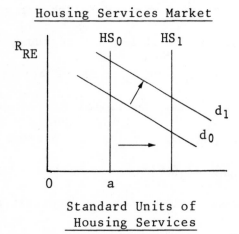

Standard Units of
Housing Services

Residential Construction Market

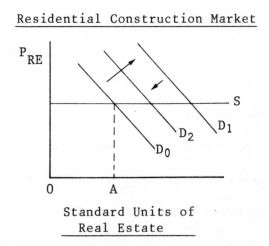

Standard Units of
Real Estate

The theoretical stationary state level of output of construction (OA) represents replacement sufficient to keep the capital stock intact and thus delivering a constant level of housing services (Oa in the housing services market). Any change in factors affecting demand for housing services (shifting demand from, say, d_0 to d_1) first changes the rental price per unit of services--and hence the asset or bid price, then changes housing starts (D_0 to D_1), and in turn the housing stock and thus the quantity of housing services (HS_0 to HS_1). The change in the stock induces change in the rental rate and thus the asset price, and in turn starts (D_1 to D_2) in the direction opposite to the initial movement. Thus, nonreplacement new real estate production takes place in response to stock disequilibrium.

Construction Inputs Market

The production function for residential construction is perhaps the least studied aspect of the housing market. Estimates of production functions for the entire construction sector are few, and no one to our knowledge has estimated a production function for residential construction itself. Indeed, until the 1972 revision of the Standard Industrial Classification, residential construction was not separated from the rest of the construction sector, which has particularly handicapped empirical work.

In theory, a complete model would specify different production functions for different types of residential construction for two reasons. First, technologies differ among types, as noted above. Second, substitutibility of inputs between types may be hindered by institutional barriers such as building codes and union rules, as well as by skill differences. Furthermore, factors are not fully mobile geographically, between residential and nonresidential construction, or between construction and other employment, which also affect input supply elasticities. Particularly, land capital is immobile, and shifting land among alternative uses is usually subject to legal constraint. There is some evidence, however, that construction labor is fairly mobile (see Swan (F42)).

In dealing with construction inputs, many models use a single construction cost index, exogenously introduced. The use of the Boeckh residential index is the most common. Occasionally, labor and materials costs appear directly (for example, see Kartman (D3), McDonough (C9), and Pollock (D5)). National models often determine the cost price endogenously, but without detailed construction input independent variables.

Mortgage Market

The effective mortgage interest rate, which is the relevant cost of capital in the housing sector, links the mortgage market to the demand for real estate production. Demand for mortgage credit is derived from the demand for real estate production and the demand for existing real estate assets. An increase in the demand for real estate production occasioned, say, by an increase in the demand for housing services, unequivocally yields an increase in the demand for mortgage credit. On the other hand, an increase in the asset price of real estate occasioned by a supply side change may or may not increase the demand for mortgage credit depending on the elasticity of demand for real estate production. In other words, rising real estate prices do not necessarily mean increased demand for mortgage credit.

Increased demand for real estate production and thus for mortgage credit will--given a less than infinitely elastic supply of credit--drive up interest rates or cause other credit rationing to occur. These changes in financing conditions affect all potential borrowers, including those who wish to purchase existing real estate. The mix of real estate on which loans are made may change. In particular, credit restrictions may affect purchases of existing real estate relative to new real estate.

The supply of mortgage credit is a much studied but still quite controversial area. Extensive consideration of supply characteristics would lead beyond the intended scope of this survey. A useful recent survey of the literature is Kearl, Rosen, and Swan (A7), (A7a). The simplest assumption is that the supply of credit is perfectly elastic at the going market rate, appropriately adjusted for risk. This assumption implies that there is no segmentation in capital markets. In turn, the implication is that general monetary policy can influence mortgage rates through its influence on interest rates throughout the economy, but that policies aimed specifically at the mortgage market will not influence mortgage rates.

In fact, in the short run, it appears that the elasticity of supply of mortgage credit is less than infinite. Flows of funds into intermediaries (particularly S&Ls and MSBs) which supply a large proportion of mortgage credit are sensitive to capital market conditions. Many models deal with these flows. Financial models (Bosworth-Duesenberry (B2), Hendershott (B9), Silber (B15)) are designed especially to deal with such flows. Other models (for example, MPS (B13) and DRI (B7)) are also equipped to differentiate among financial intermediaries. For a housing sector model emphasizing financial flows, see Sparks (C13).

Evidence of less than perfectly elastic supply is suggested by the fact that differentials between mortgage yields and yields on competing investments change with credit market conditions. Several models--notably Evans (B18a), and subsequent versions of the Wharton quarterly model--use an interest rate differential as the credit variable in their housing starts or residential investment equation. Further evidence that the supply curve is somewhat inelastic is suggested by the fact that policies designed to augment the flow of funds to mortgage markets, particularly FHLBB advances and FNMA purchases, appear to be successful in the short run. Discussions of studies examining these policies appear in Section IV of this paper.

It has been hypothesized that supply conditions differ by type of mortgage: FHA, VA, and conventional. The first two entail somewhat less risk to the lender, but in return carry insurance premiums, ceiling interest rates, or other institutional burdens. Several papers (for example, Brady (C2), (C3), and Huang (C6)) present work disaggregated along these lines. Both find significant differences between the government and the nongovernment sectors. For example, Brady (C2) finds that conventional construction varies inversely with the cost of mortgage credit, but that FHA housing is relatively unaffected by FHA mortgage yields.

The interaction of the supply and demand for credit determines the equilibrium interest rate, which, in turn, affects real estate production as described above. Disequilibrium in the mortgage market as a result of incomplete adjustments of the mortgage rate to changes in supply or demand will result in credit rationing in the case of excess demand, which will constrain the housing stock adjustment process described above. There is no reciprocal effect in the case of excess supply, of course. This asymmetry in disequilibrium in the mortgage market is emphasized by Fair (A2), (B8).

Analysis of Market Changes

To increase understanding of the relationship among the markets described above, we describe the effects in the real estate production market of changes in selected variables in a comparative statics framework, and then briefly examine market disequilibrium dynamics.

Comparative Statics

In a stationary state the stock of real estate, the equilibrium level of vacancies, and the replacement level required to maintain the stock are all constant. The rate of residential construction is sufficient to meet replacement requirements. We begin by describing changes in factors affecting the demand (or bid price) for the construction of real estate in this state, assuming the supply of mortgage credit is perfectly elastic at the going mortgage interest rate, and that supply in the real estate construction market is perfectly elastic at the going supply price. Consider changes in factors affecting the demand for housing services. For example, an increase in income will drive up the rental rate on real estate and draw vacancies down to below equilibrium levels. The resulting gap between bid price and cost price, together with the decrease in vacancies, stimulates residential construction. Builders' response, by adding to the stock, will after some period drive the asset price back to its initial level. The effects of changes in the prices of competing goods, demographics, or other taste factors are equivalent.

Changes in other factors affecting the bid price can be traced in a similar manner. A decrease in property taxes (or increased tax concession to interest payments under the income tax), which is equivalent to a decrease in the cost of capital relative to the rate of return on the stock at the margin, will drive up the bid price and stimulate construction. The increased stock will in the long run permanently drive down the rental price of real estate. The marginal rate of return in equilibrium will thus be lower than before the tax change, and the asset price of real estate will revert to its initial level. Similarly, a decrease in the interest rate resulting from a change in the mortgage market will also drive up the bid price and stimulate construction. In turn the increased stock will drive down the rate of return until the bid price has returned to its initial level.

In sum, given the assumption of a perfectly elastic supply of real estate production, demand side changes alter the asset price of housing in the short run (which may be quite long, given durability), but not in the long run. They alter the size of the stock in the long run, and also alter the rate of investment in real estate production to the extent that the larger stock requires a greater rate of replacement investment. The rental rate for housing services may or may not change in the long run, depending on the nature of the demand side change.

Changes in the cost price of real estate will, on the other hand, alter the steady state asset price of housing. For example, an increase in the cost price due, say, to increased labor costs not offset by advances in productivity, reduces the rate of return on the marginal investment in real estate production, thus inducing a reduction in the rate of replacement of the existing stock which, in turn, ultimately reduces the size of the stock and drives up the rental rate on housing services. The rate of return on investment reverts to its initial level, but the rental rate on services and the asset price reach equilibrium at higher levels.

Let us now relax the assumption of a perfectly elastic supply of mortgage credit, and assume instead that it is somewhat inelastic in the long run. The conclusions regarding the steady state in the real estate production market are not fundamentally changed. An increase in the demand for housing services drives up rental rates and draws down vacancies. The resulting increased demand for real estate production in turn stimulates the demand for mortgage credit. If the supply of credit is less than infinitely elastic, the mortgage rate rises which moderates the demand for new residential construction in any period. Neither the supply price of new production, nor the steady state stock equilibrium are altered, however. The disequilibrium created by the increase in the demand for housing stock services is corrected by investment in real estate production. The new steady state equilibrium involves a greater rate of investment than the previous steady state, and thus greater demand for mortgage credit, only to the extent that the replacement rate is greater as a result of the larger stock. A greater steady state rate of investment, given inelastic supply of credit, entails a permanently higher mortgage rate. Otherwise, the inelastic supply of credit merely alters the speed of adjustment to the new equilibrium level (which is obviously an important real world consideration). Credit rationing similarly alters the speed of adjustment, but not the underlying asset price, equilibrium stock, or equilibrium flow of new real estate production.

Next let us relax the assumption of the perfectly elastic supply of real estate production. Increased demand for housing services creates a stock disequilibrium and stimulates construction. The inelastic supply of real estate production reduces the speed of adjustment to the new stock equilibrium reducing the rate of real estate production in any period by reducing the rate of return on new production at the margin of that period. As in the case of the supply of mortgage credit described above, the new steady state asset price of housing and the stock equilibrium are altered only to the extent that a different volume of replacement investment is required.

It is important to understand firmly the essentially comparative static analysis described above to make sense out of the several strands in the literature. To begin with, the literature on the determinants of residential construction in the long run is demand oriented. In a growing economy, in the long run construction is viewed as adding to a growing equilibrium stock.

The growth of this equilibrium stock depends on the growth of demand for housing services, which is primarily a function of demographics, although other demand variables theoretically play a role. Numerous studies of long cycles in construction in general exist. Indeed, the existence of construction cycles is one of the most widely documented aspects of the "long swing," or Kuznets Cycle, hypothesis. For a brief survey of that literature, see Hickman (B10a). Esterlin (F14) contains an extensive bibliography on the subject. Campbell (F5) concentrates on long cycles in residential construction in particular, and finds that the growth in the housing population (i.e., those over 15 years of age) and changes in its age composition exert the major influence on residential construction in the 1870-1950 period. Stern (F41) applies spectral analysis to search for long cycles in residential construction, including population, immigration, and the number of marriages among his variables. He finds the long-run relationship between immigration and housing starts particularly strong. See also Marcin (F31), who estimates future housing activity to the year 2020, concentrating almost exclusively on demographics. Among the current national models, the Hickman-Coen annual model (B10) pays most attention to demographic factors.

Disequilibrium Dynamics

Adjustment to long-run equilibrium takes a great deal of time, given asset durability. Most models surveyed are concerned with short cycles in housing. They deal with quarterly or occasionally monthly data, and attention is directed toward short-run adjustment variables. In contrast to the long-run literature, this literature is not demand oriented. In particular, demographic factors are largely ignored. For example, Fromm (A3) notes the complete lack of demographic variables in seven of the ten models he surveys.

As we noted above, several papers do report the use of these variables, but the researchers do not find them empirically important.

The short-run rate of real estate production, given stock disequilibrium, may be constrained by: (1) cost and availability of financing as reflected by mortgage interest rates, other mortgage terms, and credit rationing without regard to rates or terms; (2) inelasticity of the supply of construction inputs; (3) builder perceptions of and expectations regarding the stock disequilibrium; and (4) lags in demand adjustment--demand for housing services may be a function of lagged determinants, reflecting the fact that consumers take time to adjust to income and relative price changes. The rate of production is also affected by the period of construction. The average period for single-family unit construction is about four months; for multifamily, about nine months. Site acquisitions and land development, which are in fact part of the real estate production process, will lengthen considerably the periods noted for certain types of construction.

Most short-run models surveyed assume either that financing constrains the adjustment process, or that builder expectations, which also may depend on the state of the mortgage market, are controlling. Cost or availability of credit variables, or occasionally both, in fact appear in nearly every model, and some models are concerned almost exclusively with credit variables (for example, Brady (C2)). Most researchers regard credit as the key to the short cycles, and a large measure of research effort has been directed toward the way in which the mortgage market influences the flow of residential construction. However, one analyst, Allan Meltzer, has argued in a number of papers (Arcelus-Meltzer (C1) is the main empirical work) that the availability of mortgage credit plays no role in residential construction, and that mortgage market policy directed at increasing its supply is misconceived.

Kearl, Rosen, and Swan (A7a) contend that the difference between Meltzer's position and that of others can be reconciled in large measure by distinguishing carefully between short-run adjustment behavior and long-run equilibrium. Arcelus and Meltzer use a very long time series of annual data instead of the quarterly data used by most others. Kearl, Rosen, and Swan note (p. 98),

> It is unlikely that few, if any, of the researchers who found evidence of credit rationing would argue that the availability of mortgage credit would have a substantial impact on the long-run equilibrium size of the housing stock. They are instead more concerned with cyclical fluctuations and feel that the availability of mortgage credit is an important short-run constraint.

It should be noted with regard to this controversy that Arcelus-Meltzer do find residential construction to be very interest elastic. Rising interest rates induce postponement of all durables purchases, including housing, and falling interest rates encourage purchases. Credit does, then, play a role, but the composition of credit does not. "[M]oney and credit are fungible. Loans given for one purpose can be used for another, and there is no necessary or expected relationship between the composition of credit and the composition of output." (Arcelus-Meltzer, p. 93.) Meltzer denies that policies directed at the mortgage market in particular have even a short-run effect on residential construction of any significance.

If availability of financing is the key constraint in the short run on real estate production, one can view the supply of financing as the short-run supply of real estate production. This is done explicitly in the models of Fair (B8) and Swan (C15), who estimate the supply and the demand for housing starts with arguments in the supply function being mortgage interest rates and flow of mortgage funds variables, plus time. One could, of course, specify the short-run supply of real estate production in terms of any other variable that one believed was the key constraint. For example, if one believed the supply of construction labor available to the residential sector to be the constraining factor, one could model the supply of construction labor as the short-run supply of real estate production.

One final point: models which purport to explain short-run stock adjustment behavior should be able to reflect disequilibrium in some or all markets. Most models allow implicitly or explicitly for stock disequilibrium but according to Fair (A2), few adequately provide for disequilibrium in the mortgage market.

Policies Affecting the Housing Sector

Policies designed to affect the housing sector directly affect one of the four component blocks described above. Our final task in the theory section of the survey is to categorize various policies which have either been implemented in the United States or have been proposed in the literature. Some have been analyzed in models; others have not.

Housing Services Market

Policies affecting the housing services market largely affect the demand side. Policies include general income redistribution, general stabilization policies, population policies, rent control, and tax provisions. The effect of an income redistribution policy on the demand for housing services and, in turn, on residential construction, depends mainly on the income elasticity of demand of the recipients as compared with that of the donors, although the redistribution may also affect the rate of removals from the stock and thus the rate of investment in that way. Housing allowances, which as usually proposed have a substitution effect as well as an income effect for recipients, would presumably have stronger aggregate effects on the demand for housing services than general income redistribution. The short-run effects on the rental price of real estate would be greater, and the ultimate effect on the volume of real estate production would be greater.

General stabilization policies affect the demand for housing services through their effect on income. It should be noted that one prominent stabilization tool, income tax cuts, will stimulate increases in income and, in turn, demand for housing services, but will also decrease the relative rate of return on real estate, since housing receives significant income tax concessions. Similarly, policies which inflate the economy will increase the relative rate of return in the housing sector by moving taxpayers into higher tax brackets and thus increasing the relative value of the tax concessions. We shall discuss tax policies further below.

Population policies affect the long-run demand for housing services. Campbell (F5) notes the importance of immigration in explaining residential construction in the long run. In addition, policies affecting family size and household formation will affect the demand for housing services and, in turn, real estate production.

Rent controls may reduce the rental rate on real estate and, by thus reducing the relative rate of return, will reduce the rate of construction and ultimately the size of the stock. On the supply side, the service mix delivered by state and local governments affects the supply of services provided by a given stock. State and local housing codes also affect the supply of services from a given stock and perhaps also the rate of removals from the stock.

Let us turn to various tax provisions. Taxes alter the cost of capital and thus the asset price of housing, which is to say they affect the demand for additions to the stock of real estate. Income taxes affect returns to all assets. Of particular interest here are those provisions which differentiate between housing and other assets. Under the federal personal income tax (and most state and local income taxes), property taxes and mortgage interest payments are deductible. This would square with the tax treatment of returns to other assets save for the fact that the imputed income from owner-occupant's investment in the house is untaxed. As with any deduction, the value of these deductions to the taxpayer rises with the marginal tax rate. Hence, the higher the personal income tax rate, the higher the relative rate of return on real estate. Fair and Jaffee (B13b) analyze the stimulative effect of a personal tax rate _increase_ using the MPS model. In addition, housing is afforded special capital gains treatment in the form of postponement of tax on the rollover of owner-occupied property, plus the limited forgiveness of tax on capital gains made on the sale of a principal residence after the age of 65. On the other hand, depreciation for tax purposes is not allowed on owner-occupied property. However, such allowances are allowed on rental property, and historically the allowances have been particularly generous relative to actual depreciation, so that owners have been able, in effect, to convert ordinary income into capital gains. This is accomplished by taking large depreciation allowances (thus reducing taxable income from the property), selling the property for more than its depreciated value, and paying capital gains tax rates on the sales price in excess of the depreciated value. So called "recapture" provisions limit, but do not eliminate, these tax advantages under current law. Taubman and Rasche (D7) analyze some effects of depreciation and capital gains treatment on investment in multi-family units.

In addition to income taxes, local property taxes affect the cost of capital, and thus the asset price of housing. Higher taxes raise the cost of capital, thus reducing bid prices and, in turn, the rate of production of real estate and, ultimately, the stock.

Real Estate Production Market

Demand for real estate production is derived from the demand for housing services. In a sense, it does not exist separately from the other market, and policies which affect demand for housing services also affect the demand for real estate production. One policy we list here rather than above with other federal tax provisions is the 5 percent tax credit on the purchase of newly constructed houses employed temporarily in 1975. This policy was designed specifically to increase the demand for real estate production directly, not indirectly through the demand for housing services.

On the supply side, there are numerous federal programs which subsidize housing starts, some sponsored by HUD, others by USDA. Swan (C15b) and others have examined the effects of these subsidies on real estate production. There are also programs for the rehabilitation and alteration of existing structures. The direct subsidization of construction costs is sometimes proposed. (Fair and Jaffee (B13b) analyze the effects of such a policy.) Finally, there are numerous local regulations—building codes, large-lot zoning, prohibition of mobile homes—that affect the supply of real estate production by setting minimum standards for new dwellings.

Construction Inputs Market

Meltzer (F15) suggests several policies that would directly affect construction inputs and, in turn, the supply of real estate production: increase the use of available technology by the construction industry; expand the quantity of trained, productive factors; and weaken the labor monopolies that restrict output. Others have made similar proposals. The monopoly power of unions is exercised to restrict the use of capital intensive methods--particularly the use of items produced away from the building site, and to restrict union membership. The main sources of union strength, according to Meltzer, are state and local building codes and regulations which restrict by law the substitution of capital for labor.

Mortgage Market

Many policies designed to help housing have been directed at the mortgage market. The policy interest is reflected in the literature. Policies attempt primarily to expand the supply or to reduce the price of credit (the two objectives are, of course, closely related). Those directed at supply include:

(1) Four public intermediaries--FNMA, GNMA, FHLBB, FHLMC--operate to expand the flow of funds into financial intermediaries which do most of their lending in the mortgage market. The assumption behind this activity is that the supply of mortgage credit is less than perfectly elastic. Thus, the expansion of supply, if it can be achieved, makes more credit available at the going mortgage rate (if there is nonprice rationing in the market), or drives the mortgage rate down. The lower rate reduces the cost of capital and causes the asset price of housing to be bid up, in turn increasing the rate of real estate production. Numerous studies have examined the effectiveness of these institutions (for example, Jaffee (B13g), Silber (F40), and Rosen-Kearl (C12)).

(2) Regulation Q, in effect, maintains the differential between the rates that thrift institutions and commercial banks can pay on time deposits. This differential results in a larger flow of funds to thrifts than would

otherwise occur. Since thrifts are the primary institutions in the mortgage market, it is said in turn that the flow of mortgage funds is larger than it otherwise would be. If the supply of credit is larger, the effect on real estate production is similar to that described above. Of course, mortgage flows are larger only to the extent that the inflow is not offset by an outflow of funds seeking higher returns in other sectors. Thrifts are largely confined by law to mortgage investment. However, other mortgage lenders, particularly life insurance companies, are not so constrained. There is also a ceiling on rates which S&Ls can pay on time deposits which may work to reduce the flow of funds to the mortgage market relative to what it otherwise would be.

Those directed at the price of credit include:

(1) FHA and VA interest rate ceilings and other provisions relating to FHA and VA guaranteed loans. Government loan guarantees presumably make loans less risky to lenders which will cause them to lend more cheaply. The quantity of mortgage credit demanded will then be greater, since the cost of capital is lower and, in turn, presumably the rate of real estate production is increased. The interest rate ceilings do not contribute to this effect. First, the ceilings are not binding to the degree that points paid adjust the lender's return. Further, to the extent that the ceilings are effective in holding down the price of credit through, for example, legal limitations on points paid, they increase the quantity of credit demanded, but do not increase, and probably reduce, the quantity of credit supplied. The effect on the level of real estate production is, in turn, zero or negative.

(2) State Usury Laws. These laws seek to hold down the cost of credit. To the extent that they are effective, they increase the quantity of credit

demanded but reduce the quantity supplied.

Numerous proposals have been made recently to introduce new mortgage instruments. These are designed to make mortgages more attractive to lenders (and thus to increase the supply of mortgage credit), and also to make borrowing cheaper. Among the proposals are: graduated payment mortgages and variable rate mortgages; constant-payment factor, variable-rate and price-level-adjusted instruments (PLAM). Jaffee and Kearl (B13c) have published the most extensive econometric analysis of the probable effects of these instruments.

The 1971 Report of The Hunt Commission recommends numerous changes in government regulation of all financial intermediaries. A number of proposals would have important effects on S&Ls and other mortgage lenders, and thus would probably affect the supply of credit in mortgage markets. The proposals include elimination of Regulation Q and the use of variable rate mortgages, discussed above, and also: (1) the extension of various service functions of savings institutions; (2) the extension of lending powers of savings institutions; (3) flexible loan rates on policy loans of life insurance companies. Fair and Jaffee (B13b) analyze these proposals using the MPS model.

In addition to the above policies, direct mortgage subsidies paid to lenders or to borrowers have been proposed. These would expand the volume of mortgage lending even if the supply of mortgage credit were perfectly elastic.

II. HOUSING DATA

Model specification is a function of underlying theory and available data. Data availability has particularly constrained modeling in the national housing sector. In this section, we discuss in turn the types of data available to examine each of the four markets: housing services, real estate production, construction inputs, and mortgage credit.

Overview

It was almost standard in published empirical work in the early 1960s to include a section in a paper complaining about the availability and quality of data. The number of available data series has increased considerably since 1970, which will allow analysts to specify models more completely and accurately. The most important single addition is the Annual Housing Survey (Current Housing Reports (CHR) Series 150, 151, 170, and 171) begun in 1973 and now available for 1974 and 1975.

There are nested sets of compatible data available. The data can be viewed at five levels: decennial, triennial, annual, quarterly, and monthly.

The richest detail, particularly at the metropolitan and submetropolitan levels, is available decennially in the Census of Housing (first taken in 1940). Indeed, this is the major source of data for estimation of metropolitan models.

Triennially, data will be available for selected SMSAs in the CHR-170 series, Annual Housing Survey--Housing Characteristics for Selected Metropolitan Areas. A rotating sample of 60 areas is surveyed such that data is to be collected and published on each area every three years. The first reports in the series, for 1974, are now available.

Annual data in considerable detail for the nation as a whole and for four regions are available in the CHR H-150 series (since 1973). While CHR H-150 is a richer data base than was previously available, there are a number of annual series with a long history. For example, housing starts data are available from 1889 (see Housing Construction Statistics, 1889 to 1964).

Most of the models surveyed are quarterly. Many key quarterly series extend back to 1959 or earlier, but several are available for less than a decade (for example, Current Construction Reports (CCR) series C-22 Housing Completions Data begins in 1968). The Federal Home Loan Bank Board maintains a data bank of some 80 series from 1952:2, some of which had to be constructed from more than one source in order to be available from 1952 (see Brady (Gc)2). Few geographically disaggregated data are available quarterly, although there are some regional series. A new example is CCR C-21 series New Residential Construction in Selected Standard Metropolitan Statistical Areas (first available for 1973:1).

Finally, some models surveyed use monthly data (for example, Fair (B8), McDonough (C9), and Lin (C8)). A limited number of monthly series are available from 1959 or earlier. The only geograpically disaggregated data are on number of units authorized by building permits (CCR C-400).

In addition to the data sources which are available serially at these five levels, special surveys have occasionally been done--for example, 1956 National Housing Inventory.

Obviously, smaller subsets of data are available as one filters down through the five levels. Models and their time periods are restricted by this filter. Time series models are inevitably more restricted in their choice of variables than are cross-section metropolitan models which rely primarily on data from the decennial Census. In the remainder of this section we shall discuss data in relationship to the theory outlined in the previous section, examining each of the component blocks.

Housing Services Market

In the housing services market, the relevant quantity variable is a unit of housing services, standardized for space and quality. In metropolitan models, there has been considerable effort devoted to constructing this variable (see for example, deLeeuw and Struyk (F12) pp. 62-70); in national models, the issue has been ignored. A common procedure is to assume that both the supply and the demand for the flow of housing services is proportional to the housing stock. The desired stock is not observable, but is a function of the variables that determine the demand for housing--relative prices, incomes and demographic factors, which are discussed below. The actual stock is observable. The stock may be measured in terms of numbers of dwelling units or in terms of value of stock. The assumption that the flow of services is proportional to the actual stock, as measured by the number of units, is not strictly correct for two related reasons: (1) the size and quality of units, and thus their ability to deliver services, obviously vary enormously; and (2) depreciation, alterations, additions, and maintenance affect the ability of the stock to deliver housing services, without necessarily affecting the number of units in the stock. The assumption of direct proportionality is a more reasonable one when the stock is measured in dollar terms, since the value of a unit reflects its flow of services--size and quality are taken into account. However, the flow of services is also affected by operating inputs, for example, consumer durables. These are to some extent substitutible for the stock in providing a flow of services. Thus, even when the stock is mesured in value terms, the assumption of direct proportionality of the flow to the stock is an approximation. The reasonableness of the assumption depends on the degree of substitutibility.

Data series of the housing stock and flow variables which affect it--removals, starts, depreciation, additions, and alterations--have not been, except for starts, conveniently available. Annual inventory figures are available beginning in 1973 in CHR H-150 series, Annual Housing Survey. Previous stock figures of number of units are available in the decennial Census. An inventory was also taken in 1956 (1956 National Housing Inventory). An extended series of value of stock figures, recently available, is based on fixed residential capital formation components of the gross national product (GNP) in BEA, Fixed Non-Residential Business and Residential Capital in the U.S., 1925-1975. Many researchers have constructed annual or quarterly stock series using Census data as benchmarks. The common approach is to accumulate starts, which must be adjusted in some way for removals (for example, DRI (B7)), or to accumulate investment in residential construction (for example, Wharton Mark IV (B18)). Stock estimates have also been made by using the ratio of households to occupancy rate (for example, Swan (C15)). A household is defined as a group of people occupying a dwelling unit. Data are available from Current Population Reports (CPR) P-25. Occupancy rates are available in CHR H-111 Housing Vacancies. Number of units may be converted to value of stock using some average unit price. The price should represent existing units, and not just new units. Value per unit figures are available in the decennial Census and in the new CHR H-150 series. For interim years, FHA and VA valuation figures are available (Gb15), but are not representative of the entire stock. There are other possibilities, none completely satisfactory. Construction costs, value of new houses sold, and the capitalized value of rents have been used. Bhatia (Gc1) uses the University of Michigan Survey of Consumer Finances, which provides some value data; Krekorian (D4) uses realtors' records for his study of Pomona, California. The latter approach is promising, but no national data base exists. House price data are discussed further below.

We noted that removals, depreciation, and additions and alterations affect the size of the stock in terms of its ability to deliver services. All of these factors are presumably reflected in value figures, while only removals are reflected in number of unit figures. Whether data on these are specifically needed in a particular model depends on the method of estimating the stock which is being used. An allowance for removals is necessary if stock is to be estimated by accumulating starts. Removals is an area in which data have been poor (see, for example, discussion in Ricks ed. ((F39) p. 169). The decennial Census provides extensive removals data. Few annual data have been directly available until the publication of the CHR H-150 series. Another series, CCR C-45, new in 1975, provides annual data on dwelling units authorized for demolition in permit-issuing places. Of course, demolition is not the only source of removal. Other sources, for example, conversion to nonresidential space, also exist. A common approach to adjusting for removals is to assume a fixed rate of removals (for example, DRI (B7b)).

In a value of stock estimate, depreciation can be construed to encompass both decline in the value of units and the outright removal of units from the stock. Rates of economic depreciation are notoriously difficult to construct in any area of economics. They are particularly difficult to construct in housing when not just the characteristics of the structure, but also neighborhood characteristics, affect depreciation. Two models which include a depreciation rate in a stock estimate are the Wharton Mark IV model, which uses a capital consumption allowance for real estate (from unpublished BEA data), and MPS, which estimates additions and alterations in combination with depreciation, deriving the parameters from a current expenditures on housing equation (see Kalchbrenner (B13d)). Additions and alterations also affect the ability of the stock to deliver services. The CCR C-50 series, Residential Alterations and Repairs, provides data on a quarterly basis. The quarterly series is to be discontinued in 1977. The annual series will be continued.

The demand for housing services--or, what is to say the same thing, the desired stock of housing, if we assume the proportional relationship between the stock of housing and the flow of services--is a function of demographic factors, income, prices of other goods, and the price per unit of flow of services, or price per unit of desired stock. Data on demographic factors are widely available. Population by age group and number of households, the most often used set of demographic variables, is available in CPR P-20 and P-25 series. Headship rates, defined as the proportion of the population that heads households, is a constructed variable used by several researchers. Headship rates are a function of the age distribution of the population, and also perhaps of other demographic variables--marital status, race, etc. Historically, headship has also been a function of per capita disposable income. The Campbell (F5), Marcin (F31), and Hickman-Coen (B10) models use headship rates. Current income data are, of course, widely available, and often used. Permanent income, which is not directly observable, is a more theoretically correct income concept. Several permanent income proxies have been used, including Friedman's original formulation (by Muth (C11)) and real consumption expenditure adjusted to reflect services yielded by stocks of durables instead of expenditures on new durables (MPS (B13) and Rosen-Kearl (C12)). Prices of other goods are measured by the Consumer Price Index (CPI) or the GNP deflator. The most common price of housing services variable is the rent component of the CPI. The difficulty with the use of this variable, apart from the assumption that it represents the price of a standardized unit, is that it is based primarily on multi-family rentals, while the price required includes the implicit rental rate on owner-occupied housing, as well. The implicit price deflator for rent on nonfarm dwellings is another frequently used variable. Some models (MPS (B13) and BEA (B4)) avoid the use of a rental price variable by assuming the market for housing services clears in the short run and that the stock (and hence the supply of services) is fixed. Then rent can be expressed as:

$$R_{RE} = f(KH, Y, P_o, DEM),$$

with the terms defined as before. The role that the rental price plays in a starts equation is then filled by the variables, all observable, on the right side above.

Finally, let us turn to vacancies. Vacancy data for available and unavailable units are published quarterly in CHR H-111 series. In order to assess the adjustment process in the housing services market, a measure of equilibrium available vacancies is needed. Some analysts, particularly Maisel (C10), have constructed this concept by observing the long-term trend in the vacancy rate. Cross-section studies have noted that "normal" vacancy rates differ across areas (see Winger (F45)).

Real Estate Production Market

In the real estate production market, as in the housing services market, the relevant quantity variable is in terms of standardized units, each of which provides a standard flow of services. Standard units are not directly observable and few have attempted to construct such a variable. (See Krekorian (D4) for one attempt for a single city.) One analyst (Kartman (D3) uses square feet per FHA start times total starts. A similar approach would be possible using data from the CCR C-20 series (Housing Starts). Most models seek to explain the number of starts, the value of starts, or investment in residential construction. For national models, both starts and investment in residential construction are often the output. Starts are usually an input into the determination of investment in residential construction, but not always. They are not, for example, in the Michigan model (B14). Data on number of starts are published quarterly in CCR C-20, and are available annually for nearly 100 years although the data are not fully compatible. Value of starts figures, such as are used as dependent variables in the MPS model (B13), are not published, but are available from Census. These figures represent average expected cost price upon completion of units started times number of starts. Data for single-family homes are published in CCR-25, New One Family Houses Sold and For Sale.

Number of starts is not a fully satisfactory output in terms of theory as explained above. It is subject to the same criticism levels as the use of number of units to measure the stock, above. The stock is in fact heterogeneous, as is the mix of starts at any time. A stock disequilibrium elicits an increase in the number of starts from the real estate production sector, but the number depends on the value per start. A number of large, expensive (nonstandard) units is equivalent, in terms of standard units, to a large number of small, inexpensive units. In fact, in the extreme, the real estate production sector could produce more standard units through renovation and addition without any change in the number of starts (actual new units) at all.

Value of starts is not subject to the same criticism. Value per unit will change if larger, higher quality units are constructed, but an increase in aggregate value will still reflect an increase in real estate production and, in turn, in the quantity of services delivered. Value per start also changes when the price of housing is bid up (or down). Since the desired output is a measure of production, the value figure must be deflated. For one example, the MPS model uses the Boeckh index of construction costs as the deflator (B13).

Investment in residential construction encompasses additions and alterations, which the value of starts, strictly speaking, does not. Additions and alterations data are published in CCR C-50. As we noted earlier, the relationship between investment in residential construction and starts depends on the production period which, in turn, depends on the mix of starts. The production period may also vary over the business cycle and with the weather. In the long run, technological change affects the period, probably differentially by type of start. Cassidy (Gc4) develops a time series approach to the starts to completion lag and compares it to the Census cross-section approach found in CCR C-30.

The choice of dependent variable affects the appropriate choice of independent demand variables. For example, both an increase in population and an increase in income stimulate the demand for housing services and, in turn, demand for real estate production. In either case, more standard units will be produced. However, the increase in population will tend to stimulate an increase in the number of units started, while an increase in income will tend to stimulate an increase in value per unit started. Long-run models assume demand as measured by demographic factors is the key determinant of stock and, in turn, of the flow of starts. Income and prices play little or no role. While it is true that every household by definition will have a housing unit, it is not true that the number of standard units is determinable by projection of the number of households, since units can change in size and quality. Changes in income and relative prices will influence size and quality. Long-run stock equilibrium and flow of real estate production, in value terms, can be translated into number of standard units, but not into number of actual units. Number of actual units is, as long-run models assume, likely to depend primarily on demographics.

According to the theory outlined in the previous section, real estate production is stimulated by: (1) an increase in demand resulting in the bidding up of the rental price of services; (2) a decrease in cost of capital, as reflected in changes in mortgage interest rates, property or income taxes, or depreciation rate; (3) increase in expected capital gains. These three all serve to increase the bid price of real estate. Production is also stimulated by (4) a decrease in the cost price of producing real estate, and (5) builder expectations of a profitable change in the ratio of the bid price to the cost price. We shall discuss in turn the availability of data for each of these. Several have in fact been discussed above. We have already noted that the CPI rent index and the GNP price deflator for rent of nonfarm dwellings are the common variables for rental price on services. Use of these is subject to the shortcoming noted above. There is no direct available measure of economic depreciation. An unpublished Capital Consumption Allowance (CCA) for Real Estate from the GNP accounts is used by Wharton

(B18). Disaggregated CCAs are not published. In any case, CCAs are not accurate measures of economic depreciation.

Both property taxes and income taxes impact the housing sector, but neither has been much considered in models surveyed here. Nominal property tax rates differ considerably across jurisdictions, even within a metropolitan area. Effective property tax rates depend on assessments as well as nominal rates. These diverse rate data are not conveniently available, and would be impractical to use in any case. A reasonable procedure is to derive a property tax rate from tax collection data, which are conveniently available in Governmental Finances or in City Government Finances. BEA and MPS use this procedure, dividing total receipts by current dollar value of the stock including land. The defect in this procedure is that some property taxes are collected on business property. Chase uses a property tax per house variable in its single-family starts equation. An effective federal personal income tax rate can also be calculated from receipts data available in the Statistics of Income published by the IRS. A better proxy would use tax receipts from homeowners and owners of rental property only, which might be estimated from Statistics of Income data on returns showing deductions for interest and for taxes. BEA and MPS models use a single effective federal personal income tax rate. Two further points with regard to income taxes: effects of the personal income tax in fact depend on the marginal tax brackets of the potential investors; state and local income taxes typically allow deductibility of interest and property taxes also. Not surprisingly, neither of these has been considered although sufficient data exist to do so.

Mortgage rate data are available in the Federal Reserve Bulletin and in Federal Home Loan Bank Board publications, as well as from other sources. A relatively long time series is available in Guttentag and Beck (Gc10).

Expected capital gains are not directly observable. Average rates of change for house prices and land prices have been used by MPS and BEA. Land price data are not readily available, however.

All of the variables mentioned thus far affect the bid price of real estate. In theory, introducing a bid price variable as the demand variable in a housing starts equation obviates the need for including the others, since the bid price is merely the capitalized value of the rental stream, adjusted for the other factors discussed. Price data for new, one-family units sold, available in CCR C-27 and CCR C-25 series, are reasonable proxies for bid price. Neither, however, is available in very long time series; they cover only single-family units; and few models surveyed appear to use these data. (Chase and the current version of BEA do apparently use them.) Some models (Huang (C5), (C6)) use average prices of new homes bought under VA loans.

On the cost side, it would be desirable to derive input costs from separately specified construction input markets. This is difficult, given data available, as we discuss briefly below in the section on the construction inputs market. Most models use an index of construction costs. The Boeckh index for residential construction, which is available in consistent series since 1915, is the most often used (published in the Construction Review). The index, which is a weighted average of wage and materials prices, is subject to two criticisms: it excludes site value and it does not adjust for changes in productivity. In the MPS model the Boeckh index is adjusted for growth in labor productivity. The other variable used in many models is the implicit price deflator for fixed investment in nonfarm residential structures.

Construction Inputs Market

Little work has been done on construction inputs markets. BLS price indices for several building materials are available, as are labor costs in construction, but, until the implementation of the 1972 revision of the Standard Industrial Classification (SIC), not for residential construction alone. Several models incorporate selected input variables, particularly labor cost. The cost and availability of construction finance to builders is also of interest, and some models have used proxies for this variable (for example, Rosen-Kearl use the prime rate plus 2 percent). The cost indices must somehow incorporate some individual input prices, of course, and other estimates of labor and materials requirements for housing have been made (Swan (F42), Dunlop-Mills (F13), Ball-Ludwig (F3)). Substitutibility among inputs within residential construction and substitution effects across construction industries have not been adequately investigated. Most models merely use a construction cost index. If the index is endogenous, it is typically based on construction labor costs, or on the general level of wages (examples include Liu-Hwa (B12), BEA (B4), and Wharton Mark IV (B18)).

Mortgage Market

Considerable mortgage market data exist in Federal Reserve, Federal Home Loan Bank Board, FHA and VA sources. Mortgage rate data exist for conventional, and for FHA and VA guaranteed loans for both new and existing structures. Data also exist for other aspects of mortgage contracts--loan to value ratio and term, and a number of models have introduced either or both of these variables (for example, Brady (C2), (C3); Huang (C6); Rosen and Kearl (C12)). Demand for mortgage credit is derived from demand for starts. There is, however, possibility of substitution of equity for mortgage debt in the financing of housing, which has been incorporated by some researchers by using the Aaa bond rate or some other proxy for the opportunity cost to borrowers (for example, MPS and Rosen-Kearl allow for this possibility). A large variety of variables has been used to represent the supply side of the mortgage market. A number of models, particularly Wharton, use the difference between long- (bond yield) and short- (prime commercial paper) term rates as a measure of tightness of credit, in lieu of the mortgage rate. Short-term rates tend to rise relative to long-term rates in boom periods, which reduces the flow of credit to the mortgage sector. Net flows of funds into institutions which lend in mortgage markets, disaggregated by type of institution, net acquisition of mortgages, disaggregated by type of institution and type of mortgage (FHA, VA, conventional), outstanding and new mortgage commitments, also disaggregated by type of institution, are among the variables available for modeling mortgage supply.

III. ESTIMATION PROCEDURES

The accuracy and usefulness of models is in part a function of estimation technique. The major issues in estimation technique as applied to models of residential construction can be grouped into three categories: the solution of simultaneous equations; issues regarding lags; and the use of spectral analysis. We shall treat each of these briefly.

Simultaneous Equations

Several simultaneous equation issues arise. First, the possibility of simultaneous equation bias is well recognized, but many researchers use ordinary least squares (OLS). Many of the models of the housing sector alone, listed in Sections C and D of the Bibliography, are only single equation, but for those that are not, a simultaneous technique is appropriate. This is particularly true for models that disaggregate by type of start, since the errors in these equations are likely to be correlated. A number of models have used two-stage least squares (2SLS). Examples include Brady (C2), (C3), Arcelus-Meltzer (C1), and Huang (C5, C6), as well as the major national models, although, as Fromm points out in his survey (A3), the housing sector in national models is commonly estimated by OLS. In fact, in national models in general, econometricians have made less use of simultaneous equation techniques recently (see Fromm and Klein (F20), pp. 377-414, and the discussion of that paper by Liu, pp. 415-418). Several models use simultaneous techniques other than 2SLS. For example, Rosen and Kearl (C12) use three-stage least squares, and Swan (C15b) notes the use of generalized least squares as well as OLS. Several researchers present results of estimating their models using both OLS and a simultaneous technique and compare the two. Usually, very little difference was observed. Examples are Brady (C3), Swan (C15b), and Huang (C6).

A second issue has been raised by Fair in much of the work he has done in the housing area. Fair criticizes (particularly in (A2), but also in other places) housing models for failing to provide adequately for disequilibrium effects, i.e., situations in which prices are sluggish in adjusting to fluctuations in supply or demand, giving rise to nonprice rationing. Particularly, he argues that disequilibrium in mortgage markets has asymmetrical effects. Excess supply in the mortgage market has little impact on construction, but a shortage of credit has strong immediate effects. Standard estimation techniques cannot easily deal with asymmetrical disequilibria. Fair and others have developed several alternatives for estimating such models--see Fair-Jaffee (B8c) and Fair-Kelejian (B8d). Fair's model (B8a, B8b, D1) employs these techniques, as does Swan (C15) in his version of the same model. A third issue, errors in variables, is not dealt with explicitly in most papers, but is implicit in the simultaneous equation methods used (but, see Rosen-Kearl (C12)).

Distributed Lags

The models surveyed use a variety of lag structures. Theory has relatively little to say about lag structures. This is basically an empirical question. Most of the models of the housing sector per se use discrete or moving average lags (examples are Maisel (C10a), Brady (C2), (C3), and Swan (C15)). Some use no lags at all (for example, Arcelus-Meltzer (C1)). National models mostly use distributed lag structures, as do some of the models of the housing sector per se. For example, the most recent version of the Brookings model (B3d) makes extensive use of Almon lags in its housing sector (see also MPS, DRI, Wharton, and BEA). Among the housing sector models, examples are Huang (C5) and McDonough (C9). Adjustment for serial correlation is another topic relating in a sense to lags. Many papers present a Durbin-Watson statistic suggestive of a serial correlation problem-- although the statistic is not a definitive test--but often make no adjustment for the problem. Among those that do make an adjustment, the most common techniques are Cochran-Orcutt (F7) and Hildreth-Lu (F27). Among those to make adjustments are Rosen-Kearl (C12), Silber (B15), VonFurstenberg-Herr (C16), Sparks (B13F), and others. Several papers have compared results with and without a serial correlation adjustment, and found little difference in most results (for example, Sparks (C13) and McDonough (C9)).

Spectral Analysis

Three papers surveyed here, Lin (C8), Cargill (F6), and Stern (F41), apply spectral analysis to housing sector variables in order to discern cyclical patterns. Spectral techniques enable the decomposition of a time series into components, each associated with a frequency or a time period (see Fishman (F18), Granger and Hatanaka (F24)). A frequency is a fraction of a cycle completed per time unit (a year, given annual data), and a period is the time (number of years, given annual data) required to complete one cycle. If a time series contains a cycle, the spectrum will show a peak centered on the frequency of that cycle. A significance test is needed to determine whether a peak occurs. Thus, Stern, using annual data for 1857 to 1970, finds a sharp peak in housing starts at a frequency of 0.067 cycles per year --in other words, a period of housing starts activity of 15 years. Spectral analysis allows the simultaneous estimation of all frequency components in a time series. "Smoothing" of the data is not necessary to discover underlying long cycles. If there are short cycles of average period 15 years, the spectrum will show relative peaks centered on each frequency. A coherence statistic enables the analyst to examine the degree of association between variables over their cycles, and a "phase shift" statistic estimates the average lead or lag of one series over another at each frequency. Spectral analysis can be integrated with multiple regression analysis, as is done by Lin (C8). Two problems must be dealt with in applying spectral techniques. First, time trends must be removed from the data through some variable transformation in order to apply the technique. Second, the number of frequency components (so called "lags") must be predetermined. If a small number of frequency components is chosen, relatively few cycles can be revealed. However, the variance of the spectral estimates and the number of frequency components are directly related. Thus, choice of a large number of frequency components allows more complete examination of the data for the presence of cycles, but the results are less statistically reliable.

IV. POLICY RESULTS

There are four basic questions to ask regarding any model: (1) What are the outputs of the model? (2) What are the inputs? (3) What are the effects of one or more inputs on the outputs? (4) What confidence can we have in the model? The scope of these questions is unfortunately too broad to address them in their generality. In this survey we focus on the effects of policy variables (some inputs) on residential construction (an output).

At the end of the theory section, we listed policies affecting the residential construction sector directly or indirectly. In this section, we shall discuss the results of policy analyses which have been performed. We will not treat in detail policies which could be, but have not been, analyzed, since such an exercise would be quite speculative. We will, however, occasionally note models which would be appropriate for analysis of a particular policy. A model is appropriate if it contains the policy variable or a reasonable proxy for it.

The results reported are not precisely comparable. Model specification and estimation periods differ. Reestimation to make results directly comparable is in itself a major research effort which is beyond the scope of this paper. (See Grebler and Maisel (A5) and Edwards (A1) for some limited efforts in this direction.) We report two types of results—coefficients for policy variables and the results of simulations of changes in policy variables. In all cases the simulations were deterministic, with little attention given to the probabilistic characteristic of the policy effects.

Models vary considerably in detail, degree of sophistication, and degree of conformance to theory as outlined above. These factors obviously affect the confidence one can have in the results. In this regard, it should be noted that results from models of the housing sector per se are, in theory, limited in reliability because they cannot allow for the full set of inter-actions with the rest of the economy. However, increasing the complexity of a model increases the possibility of serious misspecification, and, in prac-tice, the results of analysis performed in the context of a full national model may not be any more reliable (indeed, perhaps less) than results of analysis performed using a housing sector model, or the housing sector of a national model without allowing for feedbacks.

The rest of this section is organized along the lines of previous sections, discussing policies according to which component "block" is directly affected.

Housing Services Market

While the effects on the demand for housing services of various govern-ment policies we listed in the section above, particularly tax policies, have been widely discussed, there has been relatively little empirical work rela-ting these policies to residential construction. We shall focus on taxes, an area in which a few studies have been carried out.

Federal personal income tax deductions of interest and property taxes render consumption of housing services cheaper than it otherwise would be. The higher the personal income tax rate, the more attractive, relatively speaking, is the consumption of housing services. Fair and Jaffee (B13b), using the MPS model, simulate the effect on residential construction of increasing personal income tax rates across the board by 25 percent. The simulation used the full MPS model except for the "currency," employment, and labor sectors, so that feedback effects were allowed to play a role. The policy change was accomplished by altering the income tax variable in the cost of capital equation for single-family starts. This is a crude representation of the effect of a personal income tax rate change, since it is the change in the marginal rates of a selected proportion of the population that is in fact relevant, but a more detailed analysis cannot be performed, given a single average personal income tax rate in the model. The simulation period was ten years, with the initial change introduced in the second quarter of 1960, i.e., 1960:2. The stimulative effect on starts due to the substitution effect in favor of homeownership was found to be largely offset by the negative income effect of the tax increase. Note that tax cuts would have the opposite effect. Fair and Jaffee compare the results with the levels that would have been achieved if Regulation Q and other deposit ceilings for financial intermediaries had been removed. Apparently, then, the simulation of the tax increase was run assuming the removal of deposit ceilings as well. The results were an increase in the annual flow in 1970 of investment in residential construction of $1.1 billion or 3.9 percent over the level that would have been achieved had the only change been removal of deposit ceilings. The increase over the actual historical value was $0.8 billion. They also found an increase in the stock of $5.4 billion, or 0.7 percent, which is a decrease of $3.9 billion relative to the historical value.

A similar income tax exercise would be possible with the BEA model, but other models are not equipped to deal with the effects of changes in income tax provisions on residential construction. Tax variables do not appear in the housing sector equations. Other national models do, of course, contain tax variables--in some cases, a large number of them. For example, the Wharton Mark IV model contains a very detailed tax sector. In the context of the entire model, tax changes would affect housing, but there is no provision for any direct effect, nor for a differential effect relative to the consumption of other goods and services.

Effects of changes in selected tax provisions relating to rental property are analyzed by Taubman and Rasche (D7) for the apartment building industry (buildings of three or more units) using a housing sector model which conforms quite well to the theory described in Section II above. Their simulations use annual data, with exogenous variables fixed at 1963 levels. The simulations were carried out over 132 periods, and the last 14 periods are reported in the paper. Nine simulations are reported, of which six are of interest here: (1) the control simulation was one in which the original owner was allowed to double declining balance depreciation allowance, and the subsequent owners were allowed 150 percent declining balance; (2) 150 percent declining balance to all owners; (3) straight-line depreciation to all owners; (4) the same as (1) above, with "excess" depreciation taxes as ordinary income rather than capital gains; (5) the same as (1) above, except that the after-tax rate of return on alternative investments is assumed to be 12 percent instead of 5.7 percent--the value in the previous simulations; (6) the same as (3) above, with the after-tax rate of return on alternatives equal to 12 percent. The tax rate on ordinary income is assumed throughout the exercise to be 50 percent. We will compare the results in (2), (3), and (4) with those in (1).

Each of these changes increases the taxes paid on returns to investment in real estate and will reduce the flow of starts and, in the long run, the housing stock. The long-run results (average values in the last ten periods 123-132) are: the change to 150 percent declining balance reduces multifamily starts by 1.3 percent and the stock by 1.4 percent; the change to straight line reduces starts by 2.9 percent, the stock by 2.7 percent; taxing capital gains as ordinary income reduces starts by 9 percent and the stock by 6.7 percent. When the after-tax rate of return on alternatives is raised to 12 percent, comparison between simulations (5) and (6) shows a decline in starts of 5.1 percent and of the stock by 4.6 percent. The absolute sizes of both the stock and the flow are, of course, much smaller than in the comparable simulations (1) and (3). The results of changing depreciation rules may be compared with the Taubman-Rasche results for office buildings (F44). The office building results are about four times as large because double de-clining balance may be claimed by all owners for such buildings, not merely original owners. The effects of taxing capital gains on excess depreciation at ordinary income tax rates has a larger effect than allowing straight-line depreciation because even straight-line depreciation is generous relative to economic depreciation in the early years of life of an asset. The actual numerical results of Taubman and Rasche are to be taken as no more than indicative. Indeed, as they point out, one does not know whether the cyclical properties of their simulation conform at all to observed behavior. Nonetheless, their model is interesting for the tax law detail introduced.

Local property taxes impact demand for housing services. Relatively little has been done in the literature to analyze the effects of these factors on residential construction, and the detail provided in the models again does not permit much analysis without modification of the models. Fair and Jaffee (B13b) analyze the effects on residential construction of de-creasing the property tax across the board by 25 percent, using the full MPS model. The tax change was introduced by altering the exogenous property tax variable in the single- and multifamily cost of capital equations. The real time simulation period was 1960:2 to 1970:3 and the control solution assumes no ceilings on deposit rates, as in the income tax simulation discussed above. The effect on investment in residential construction is $1 billion after ten years, or 3.5 percent; on the housing stock it is $22.2 billion, or 2.7 percent. Again, a similar exercise would be possible with the BEA model, but most models contain no tax variables structured to have any direct effect on the housing sector. One exception is the Chase model (B5), in which a constructed average monthly payment variable which includes property taxes, among other things, appears in the single-family starts equation. The coefficient suggests that a $10 change in the average monthly payment gives rise to 23,000 starts.

Real Estate Production Market

There are a large number of federal subsidy programs operating under both HUD and USDA. While these obviously vary in the extent to which they impact residential construction, no model of which we are aware disaggregates among them. Swan (C15b) reports disaggregating to the extent of introducing a variable for Section 235 and 236 starts alone, but he got insignificant results. Several models introduce subsidized starts in the aggregate. Swan's paper (C15b) is devoted primarily to examining the overall impact of these programs on housing starts. Swan's model, using quarterly data, is a four-equation disequilibrium model of the type developed by Fair (B8a) in which either supply or demand operates to constrain the quantity supplied in disequilibrium. The supply equation in this model is a supply of financing equation. The supply of residential construction is assumed perfectly elastic, so that finance is the effective supply constraint. The number of subsidized starts is introduced into the demand for starts equation, and the coefficient on the subsidy variable is constrained to unity. The effect of this constraint is to assume that the subsidized units do not decrease the demand for new nonsubsidized units, an assumption which Swan describes the as "the most favorable assumption one can make about the subsidy programs" (p. 124). Swan reports results of three simulations: increase in subsidized starts of 300,000 (equivalent to roughly doubling the then existing number); decrease in subsidized starts of 300,000; holding subsidies at their 1969:1 level of 175,227. The equilibrium response in total starts to the change of 300,000 subsidized starts was only 42,000. In other words, the increase in subsidized starts is 86 percent offset by decreases in nonsubsidized starts (and vice versa). The adjustment paths of the increase and decrease differ because the increase is immediately supply constrained while the decrease makes starts demand constrained. The initial impact of the increase is very small because the inelastic supply constraint operates immediately; the impact of the decrease is a full 300,000 units immediately, and smaller decreases in subsequent years. The effect of the decrease damps rather quickly. The result of simulating subsidized starts at their 1969:1 level is similar. Through 1972:2, total subsidized starts were 593,000 fewer than were actually built, but total starts had declined by only 70,000--i.e., all but 12 percent of the decline in subsidized starts was offset by increases in nonsubsidized starts. The explanation for these results is that,

> . . . while increases in the subsidy programs increase the demand
> for new units, they do not expand the volume of mortgage fi-
> nancing. Competition for funds to finance more units increases the
> mortgage rate, which in turn reduces the demand for non-subsidized
> units. (p. 134.)

Swan concludes that subsidies may be useful policy tools for redistri-
bution, but that they should not be used as a technique for influencing the volume of starts. He notes several factors which in fact would probably

reduce further the effect of subsidies on total starts. First, the assumption that there is no substitution on the demand side, as mentioned above, is probably not true. Second, the simulations do not incorporate any changes in savings inflows into financial intermediaries, vacancy rates, or the housing stock, resulting from the simulated policy change. In accord with theory, we would expect the expanded stock resulting from an increase in subsidized starts to decrease further the equilibrium impact on total starts.

The Swan model does not conform well to the theoretical framework described above. Given the nature of the Swan model, the impact of housing subsidies will necessarily be small. If financing is the constraint, then only increases in financing will have much impact on residential construction. While this is an empirically reasonable result in the short run, it is a questionable one in the long run. Theory suggests than an increased inflow of funds into the mortgage market attracted by the relatively high returns there will mitigate the supply constraint in the long run. The long-run equilibrium impact on total starts of increasing the number of subsidized starts may be small, but the reason is more likely to be demand side substitution of subsidized for nonsubsidized units than an inelastic supply of mortgage credit. In short, the validity of Swan's conclusion should be tested in the context of other models. Few models permit such a test without respecification, however, since they do not include a variable for subsidized starts.

Two models which do introduce subsidized starts are Rosen and Kearl (C12) and DRI (B7b). Like Swan, Rosen and Kearl introduce the number of subsidized starts, defined to include the Section 235, 236, and 221(d)3 programs, into a demand for housing equation. Subsidies are viewed as "affecting the real price paid for housing." The coefficient indicates that 100,000 subsidized starts give rise to demand for 170,000 total new starts but not necessarily to 170,000 units of actual production, since production depends also on the supply side of the model. This contrasts to Swan's model in which the coefficient on the subsidy variable is confined to unity, a priori. On their own results, Rosen and Kearl "caution against a literal interpretation of the subsidy coefficient because [they] do not assume any behavioral relation other than intuitively the impact of price reduction" (p. 15).

DRI introduces the number of government subsidized starts, lagged one quarter into an equation explaining the supply of private starts including shipment of mobile homes. The coefficient appears to indicate that 100,000 subsidized starts are associated with 700,000 total starts. This figure, which seems unreasonably large, is not directly comparable to the results mentioned above. There is no separate demand equation in the DRI model.

Fair and Jaffee, in the same paper reporting the tax simulations above, simulate the impact of a number of other programs designed to directly affect residential construction, using the full MPS model. A direct subsidy of 10 percent of construction costs as viewed by the builder was simulated, as was a similar subsidy of 25 percent of the construction cost. The effect was introduced into the model by reducing the construction cost variable--Boeckh index--by the amount indicated beginning in 1960:1 in the single-family and multifamily starts equations. The simulation period was again ten years. The results were: (1) given a subsidy of 10 percent, investment in residential construction increased by $1.3 billion, or 4.6 percent--beyond what it would have been in 1970:3 given, as before, that deposit ceilings had been dropped--and housing stock increased by $20.6 billion, or 2.5 percent; (2) given a subsidy of 25 percent, investment in residential construction increased by \$2.7 billion, or 9.5 percent, and the stock increased by \$61.4 billion, or 7.5 percent. The authors point out that the efficiency of the subsidy depends on the cost of achieving the above listed increments in the stocks and flows. If it is assumed that policy makers can somehow identify and pay the subsidy only on investment that would not otherwise have taken place, the cost of the subsidy to the government would be exactly 10 percent of the increase in the stock in the case of the 1-0 percent subsidy--\$2.06 billion in ten years. On the other hand, if the subsidy is paid on all construction during the period, the cost of the 10 percent subsidy is approximately \$35.5 billion in ten years since the housing stock increased from \$485 billion in 1960 to \$840 billion in 1970--an increase of \$355 billion. In other words, under this assumption, the government must spend about \$1.75 of subsidy for each \$1 of construction instead of \$0.10 as in the first assumption. The latter calculation is in nominal terms and somewhat overstates the subsidy cost, but the difference in the two assumptions remains dramatic. There is no way, within the context of the model, to decide which of these is more correct, yet that information is obviously of major importance in assessing the viability of the policy. This exercise could be carried out using most of the models surveyed, since nearly every one contains a construction cost variable. On the other hand, no model surveyed would enable an accurate assessment of subsidy cost.

Fair and Jaffee also simulate the effect of a 10 percent subsidy of interest costs to the mortgage borrower, i.e., the government rebates 10 percent of interest costs, and a 10 percent subsidy to lenders on mortgage contracts, i.e., the lender receives 10 percent more interest than the borrower pays in the market. These policies bear a rough resemblance to some of of the subsidy programs actually in existence. The policy changes were

introduced respectively by raising the coefficients of the first four variables in the mortgage rate equation by 10 percent, and by raising the mortgage rate by 10 percent in the mortgage supply equations for each of the
principal financial intermediaries in the mortgage market. The results were
very similar. The mortgage stock increased about 17 percent--far more than
in the simulations by Fair and Jaffee that we noted above, since mortgages
became relatively attractive financial instruments. However, the flow of
investment in residential construction increases by only $0.3 billion, or
1 percent, and the stock has increased by only $4.7 billion, or 0.5 percent,
in the tenth year of the simulation. Considerable substitution between
mortgage debt and equity has taken place. The efficiency of the policy
again depends on whether the subsidy is paid on all mortgages or on the
increment induced by the policy itself. Fair and Jaffee conclude, however,
that direct subsidy of construction costs is far more efficient than subsidy
of mortgage borrowing or lending in stimulating housing investment. This
exercise could also be carried out in the context of a number of other
models, although some lack a mortgage rate variable.

Construction Inputs Market

There has been little federal policy activity directed at the construction inputs market, per se. State and local building codes, licensing pro-
cedures and the like may be regarded as having primary impact on the construction inputs market. These factors have not been dealt with in the
models reviewed here. We have noted above several suggestions by Meltzer
directed at inputs--expand the output of trained factors, increase use of
construction technology, weaken union monopolies. Models reviewed here are
not equipped to examine the effects of these sorts of policies directly

because they do not model the construction inputs sector in any detail. In most cases, about all that can be done without respecification is to examine the effect of altering the cost of construction variable as Fair and Jaffee did in the simulation of the effect of a construction cost subsidy, discussed above. Such an approach yields but a very rough indication of an input sector policy, however. The first problem lies in determining how much impact the input market policy will have on construction costs. Some models introduce a wage variable, at least, to explain the deflator for residential construction (for example, BEA (B4), Liu-Hwa (B12)). One could test the effect of altering that variable. A few papers (Pollock (D5), Kartman (D3), and Mc-Donough (C9)) deal with the supply side of residential construction, and introduce more cost of construction variables. None of these is suitable for testing policy approaches such as those of Meltzer, however. These are single-equation models designed for special purposes. There is no underlying production function.

Mortgage Market

In contrast to analysis of policies directed at other parts of the housing sector, policies directed at the mortgage market have been extensively analyzed. Most often examined is the effect of the public intermediaries which act to increase the supply of mortgage credit. There are four such intermediaries--FNMA, GNMA, FHLMC (Federal Home Loan Mortgage Corporation)--which purchase mortgage debt from primary intermediaries, and the FHLBB, which makes advances to S&Ls which can then expand their mortgage lending. FHLBB advances and FNMA acquisitions appear in many models. Most do not include FHLMC or GNMA activity separately and explicitly. DRI is an exception. Several models combine FNMA and GNMA activity in a single variable.

Most models treat the activities of the intermediaries as exogenous. This is, strictly speaking, incorrect, since the agencies operate to counteract the short-term fluctuation in residential construction. Policy makers react to changes in variables in the housing sector. Thus, the volume of FNMA and FHLBB activity is endogenous--that is, determined within the system. Three papers, Rosen-Kearl (C12), Silber (F40), and Hendershott-Villani (B9b) make both FHLBB advances and FNMA acquisitions endogenous in separate equations. The Rosen-Kearl model assumes that activity of both intermediaries is a function of savings flows to S&Ls and other intermediaries, the exponential growth trend in the volume of mortgages outstanding, and deviations from that trend. Silber estimates a number of reaction functions. FHLBB advances are modeled in two ways--one with the volume of advances as the dependent variable; and one using the rate charged on advances, which is the variable actually controlled, as the dependent variable in a separate equation specified for the demand by S&Ls for the advances made at the controlled rate. The volume of starts, the mortgage rate, savings flows, and the cost of funds to the FHLBB are the important independent variables. FNMA behavior was found by Silber to be dependent upon starts, the mortgage rate, and savings flows, with the mortgage rate most important. Hendershott's FNMA equation contains only a mortgage rate and a dummy for institutional changes. He assumes that FHLBB advances are determined not by the FHLBB, but by the S&Ls receiving the advances. Deposit inflows and the mortgage rate are the independent variables. The Bosworth-Duesenberry model (B2) also treats FHLBB advances as endogenous, but FNMA acquisitions are regarded as exogenous.

The activities of the intermediaries are introduced in several ways. A variable reflecting such activity appears in several single-equation housing starts models, for example, Maisel (C10), Swan (C14), and Brady (C2).

Several structural models which separate supply and demand for residential construction introduce FHLBB advances or FNMA net acquisitions into the supply of residential construction. This is the approach of Fair (B8) and Swan (C15), whose supply equation is the supply of financing. Utt (C16) introduces commitments under the GNMA unsubsidized tandem program into both the supply and demand equations for starts. Like Fair's and Swan's, Utt's supply equation is a supply of financing equation. Rosen and Kearl (C12) place public intermediary activity into the mortgage supply equation which is, in turn, an input into the supply of residential construction. Several models (for example, Huang (C6), MPS (B13), and DRI (B7)) introduce federal credit agency activity into both the mortgage market and directly into residential construction. Huang views the variable as influencing builders by influencing how actively financial institutions issue commitments, and thus as belonging in the supply of residential construction equation. The rationale for including changes in FNMA and GNMA purchases in the housing starts equation in the DRI model is apparently similar. MPS introduces the change in the stock of mortgages held by FNMA as part of a lagged variable representing the change in outstanding mortgage commitments of S&Ls into the single-family starts equation. The variable is viewed as a proxy for availability of short-run mortgage financing, and as a way of capturing construction financing costs which are excluded from the Boeckh index, which is the MPS construction cost variable.

We shall first discuss the results of simulations of FNMA purchases. Bosworth-Duesenberry (B2a) present the result of simulating over the period 1965:1 to 1970:2 a permanent change of $1 billion in FNMA asset holdings. The result is a $0.8 billion increase in investment in residential construction at a seasonally adjusted annual rate (SAAR) in the first half year

and about a $0.5 billion increase for all of 1965, but the change in invest-
ment in residential construction is negative in several subsequent periods,
so that the cumulative effect after six years is only $0.3 billion. The
negative effects result from the feedback of higher market rates occasioned
by FNMA borrowing to finance the mortgage purchases. The authors suggest
that the long-term effect would probably be zero. In a subsequent paper
(B2b), Bosworth and Duesenberry report a simulation over the 1969-1971 period
in which FNMA purchases are held to their 1966 growth rate, implying FNMA
holdings $10.1 billion less than they actually were at the end of 1971.
Again, residential construction is immediately sharply affected. In the
first year of the simulation period, investment in residential construction
is down $1.7 billion. Bosworth and Duesenberry conclude that FNMA purchases
do have significant short-run stabilization effects. Offsetting effects
occur with a considerable lag, with much of the lag concentrated in the
financial sector, where portfolio adjustments take place slowly. Eventually
(beyond the simulation period), the impact of FNMA purchases dissipates
completely. In evaluating the results of simulations with the Bosworth-
Duesenberry model, one should note that their purpose is to model the flow of
funds. The real sector of the model is relatively rudimentary, and the
residential construction equation, in their words, "simply translates a given
change in the mortgage stock into a corresponding amount of expenditure"
(B2a, p. 73), although in fact they do include a household formation variable
along with the financial variables.

Fromm and Sinai (B7b) report the result of simulation of a permanent
$1 billion increase in FNMA holdings using the DRI model. The simulation
period was 1962:1 to 1972:4, but results are reported only through 1964. As
in the Bosworth-Duesenberry result reported above, they find an immediate

positive impact on investment in residential construction, followed by decreases in subsequent years due to financing effect feedbacks. The initial effect is much smaller than in the Bosworth-Duesenberry model--$0.2 billion in the first quarter (SAAR) and $0.225 billion in the first year following the change. The effect has almost dissipated by the end of the third year.

Hendershott (B9a) also reports a simulation of $1 billion increase in federally sponsored credit agency (FSCA) holdings, which means primarily FNMA, occasioned by a purchase in 1969:1, using his financial model. The simulation is reported over the 1969 to 1971 period. As in the other simulations reported above, investment in residential construction overshoots-- increasing sharply at first, then declining. The effect one year after the quarter of the policy action is $0.47 billion, but after three years, the cumulative effect is $0.23 billion. He also reports the effect of approximately freezing FSCA holdings at 1965 levels. By 1971:4, this results in holdings $17.9 billion lower than actual levels. The cumulative impact on housing investment was only $4.5 billion.

Numerous other studies include FNMA activity in their estimating equations. Among these are MPS (B13), Brady (C2), Huang (C6), Maisel (C10a), Burnham (C10c), Sparks (C13), and Rosen-Kearl (C12). Still other studies (for example, Fair (B8a) and Swan (C15a)) report unsuccessful attempts to include FNMA in their models.

Edwards (A1) surveys in detail the effects of FHLBB advances on housing starts and mortgage flows in 12 models, and we shall not replicate his effort by presenting results from individual models here. He concludes that the common finding of the studies is that FHLBB advances have had significant short-run effects in the past, but that these effects may have been largely the product of the existence of credit rationing at the time the advances were made. Were the advances made when mortgage markets were in equilibrium, the effects even in the short run may have been much smaller. According to Edwards, the consensus of the studies is that a $1 billion increase in advances would boost starts by 35,000 to 40,000 in the short run in the 1960-1970 decade--20,000 at current prices--but that the long-run effect is minimal. The lack of long-run effect is predicted by theory, of course. The advances do not change the demand for housing services, the supply price of residential construction or the structure of interest rates.

Several papers (for example, Fair (B8b) and Brady (C2)) find that FHLBB advances have positive effects on starts, but that FNMA acquisitions do not. Brady (C2) suggests that the reason for this is institutional--FNMA purchases allow intermediaries to buy nonmortgage assets, while FHLBB advances go to S&Ls, which are locked into buying mortgages. Swan (C15a) suggests a different and more plausible sort of explanation. FNMA provides credit at times when intermediaries are restricting mortgage lending and when mutual savings banks are buying corporates instead of mortgages. The counter-cyclical pattern of FNMA activity produces a negative correlation between FNMA purchases and starts--a result without causal significance. Rosen and Kearl (C12) offer a similar analysis of both intermediaries. They are countercyclical, but their actions have not been strong enough to offset periodic credit stringency in the mortgage and housing markets. Thus, the authors find a positive relationship between intermediary activity and deviation of actual from target mortgage levels. Silber (F40), on the other hand, rejects the conclusion that FHLBB advances have positive effects, but that FNMA acquisitions do not, as statistically invalid. He notes the in-clusion of both variables in the same starts equation is likely to generate multicollinearity.

One paper surveyed, Fromm-Sinai (B7b), simulated $1 billion of new commitments to purchase mortgages by FHLMC. The policy change was introduced in 1971:3 and carried for six quarters. As is the case with the other simulations of credit agency activity mentioned above, there is a short-run effect on investment in residential construction and on starts, which eventually disappears. The effect on investment in residential construction in the first year is about $0.2 billion or on housing starts, about 11,000 units.

One study, Utt (C16), examines the effect on the supply of and demand for starts of GNMA commitments to purchase mortgages under the unsubsidized tandem plan first introduced in 1971:3. The model is estimated from 1961:2 to 1975:4. He finds that while one million dollars of commitments increase the demand for starts by nine units in the following quarter, they decrease the supply by 13 units. The net effect of increased tandem commitments is, then, to reduce starts. He finds positive impacts on the FHA and VA insured markets separately examined, but notes that these results may merely reflect substitution away from conventional financing arrangements. While insignificant results would not be surprising, the negative impact on starts is difficult to explain. Utt suggests that it could reflect an overreaction by lenders who shift out of mortgages into other financial assets as the increased supply of subsidized credit causes a decline in mortgage interest rates relative to other rates. One would then expect a correction in subsequent quarters. Utt was not able to find this effect, but the period of estimation of the model is relatively short.

Another policy which affects mortgage flows and has been subject to considerable analysis is the effect of Regulation Q and of ceiling rates payable on deposits by S&Ls and MSBs. The effect of Regulation Q is to maintain a lower time deposit rate in commercial banks than in savings institutions, when the ceiling is effective. Removal of Regulation Q, then, should shift deposits away from savings institutions relative to commercial banks, and since savings institutions are prime mortgage lenders, funds may, depending on the relative attractiveness of mortgages to other types of lenders, flow out of mortgage markets. Relaxing the rate ceiling on S&Ls and MSBs should conversely allow them to be more competitive, and stimulate an inflow of funds into the mortgage market. Simulations of the effects on housing starts of removing the ceilings have been performed by several researchers.

Fair-Jaffee (B13b), in the paper cited earlier, simulate the removal of Regulation Q alone, and the removal of all deposit rate ceilings, using the MPS model. The model includes the Regulation Q ceiling directly, and the authors simply raised it to a level such that it was not effective in the si-simulation period. The simulation period was 1960:1 through 1970:3, but the Regulation Q ceiling was not effective in the model (in the sense that it was historically above actual rates) before the authors altered the ceiling until 1968:1. Thus, the simulations of the policy change are in effect for the last three years only. The effect of removing Regulation Q is to reduce the housing stock by $1.8 billion by 1970:3 and to reduce investment in residential construction by $1.3 billion (SAAR) for that quarter. When deposit ceilings are also removed from intermediaries, the effects are reduced to a negligible -$0.3 billion stock effect and -$0.2 billion flow effect in 1970:3. Fair and Jaffee conclude that

> . . . the removal of deposit rate ceilings from depository institutions will have minor quantitative effects on mortgage lending and housing and even the direction of change is in doubt. (p. 114.)

Jaffee and Kearl (B13c) also use MPS to simulate the effects of removing deposit rate ceilings. The simulation period was 1962:1 to 1973:4. Only the mortgage, savings deposit and housing sectors of the model were used. The rest of the model is treated as exogenous. The results are similar to those of the Fair-Jaffee paper mentioned above. The effect on the stock of housing for the entire simulation period is +$0.1 billion. The effect is counter-cyclical with respect to investment in residential construction. Removal of ceilings appeared to stimulate investment in residential construction in slack periods in that sector and dampen it in strong quarters.

Bosworth and Duesenberry (B2b) simulate raising deposit ceilings for S&Ls, MSBs and commercial banks by 50 basis points. The shock is adminis-tered in 1969:1, and the effect is simulated for three years. The effect on the rate of investment in residential construction averaged +$2.4 billion per year after the first six months (in which the effect was at a +$0.8 billion annual rate). In other words, the results are very different from those derived from the MPS model. Note, however, that the ceiling on large certi-ficates of deposit (CD) was specifically not raised in the Bosworth-Duesenberry simulation.

Finally, Fromm and Sinai (B7b) use the DRI model to simulate an increase of 1 percent in the ceiling rates for all three intermediaries. They report the results for 1970:4 through 1972:4. Like Bosworth and Duesenberry, they find a strong positive impact on the mortgage market and, in turn, on starts and investment in residential construction. They explain this by noting that S&Ls and MSBs raise their rates almost to the new ceilings, while commercial banks raise their rates by less. They suggest that this may be true because commercial banks alter rates on large CDs and thus somewhat stem fund out-flows. Investment in residential construction is higher than the control simulation by $6 billion, or about 14 percent in 1971, and nearly $9 billion, or 19 percent in 1972. The results for starts are similar. As the authors note, the simulation is for a recession period, and the impact would be smaller if the economy were operating nearer capacity.

FHA and VA loan guarantees have historically been made on a significant portion of new housing sales. Contracts written under the guarantee programs contain a number of provisions which may affect construction. Of particular interest to researchers has been the interest rate ceilings. The effect of the ceilings on aggregate starts was widely discussed in the early 1960s (see, for example, Grebler-Maisel (A5) and Alberts (F1)). The so-called "fixed rate" hypothesis is that the ceiling, when effective, dampens the attractiveness of mortgage loans, and therefore reduces the supply of mortgage credit and, in turn, construction. The ceiling is most likely to be effective in business cycle expansions, when credit in general is tightening and interest rates are high. This ceiling on interest rates then, according to the hypothesis, explains the countercyclical pattern of starts observed in the post-World War II period. In order that the ceiling be effective, of course, the market must be unable to completely discount the ceiling effect. This inability to discount is presumably a short-run phenomenon, resulting from institutional barriers. Recent literature has paid less attention to FHA-VA ceilings and to separating the government guaranteed sector from the conventional sector (but see VonFurstenberg-Herr (C17), Brady (C3), and Lin (C8)). Since 1968, there has been much more adjustment in ceiling rates to reflect market conditions than was true in previous periods.

Two papers surveyed disaggregate the residential construction market into three sectors: FHA starts, VA starts, and conventional starts. Brady (C2) estimates the three-equation model by 2SLS and finds that the government sectors behave differently from the conventional sector. A variable representing the interest rate spread between the appropriate mortgage rate and Moody's Baa rate was introduced into each equation. It is positive in each of the government sectors and negative but insignificant in the conventional sector, suggesting support for the fixed rate hypothesis described above. Brady also rejects the notion that the FHA and VA sectors can be considered together. The importance of the explanatory variables in the two equations differs. Particularly, investment in FHA-insured housing is relatively unaffected by changes in FHA mortgage yields, while the coefficient on yield in the other sectors is negative and significant. The difference between government sectors is, in part, a function of the period of estimation: 1952:2 through 1963:2. Behavior in the government sectors has been less disparate recently, and Brady, in a later paper (C3), combines FHA and VA into one government guaranteed sector. Smith, in a comment critical of Brady's work (C2a), presents two alternative models using Canadian data, and shows that the conventional and government guaranteed sectors behave similarly. Ray Fair (A2) notes that Brady's equations are best interpreted as supply of finance equations and the implicit assumption is that demand is always sufficient to absorb the supply from the financial sector.

Huang (C6) estimates a demand for new housing, a supply of starts, and the supply and demand for mortgage credit--each type of equation disaggregated into the three sectors over the 1953:2 through 1965:4 period. Demand and starts equations are also estimated in both number of starts and value of starts terms. Like Brady, he finds differences between the government sectors, as well as between the government and conventional sectors. With respect to starts, Huang finds the spread between the ceiling and an Aa bond yield to be significant for VA starts, but not for FHA. He also reports that spreads between mortgage yields and Aa yields did not perform particularly well in any sector. In the supply of mortgage credit equation, on the other hand, he finds that the ceiling-Aa spread is significant in the FHA equation but not in the VA equation. The supply of mortgage credit is not entered into the starts equations. Huang offers no interpretation of the difference between the FHA and VA sectors in the starts and supply of credit equations. We conclude that the evidence of the validity of the fixed rate hypothesis, based on Huang's work, is at best mixed.

Sparks (C13) disaggregates by type of lender, using annual data over the 1949-1964 period. He finds the spread between the average of the VA and FHA ceilings and the Aaa rate to be a significant determinant of the supply of mortgage credit for MSBs, while the corporate rate alone was a better determinant of life insurance company lending. S&Ls were assumed not to be responsive to the ceiling-bond rate differential because their portfolio choices are restricted by law. Sparks assumes that the mortgage market clears, and the supply of mortgage credit results are thus used directly to estimate starts. The role of ceiling rates is minor, but not zero in Sparks' analysis. Using quarterly data 1952:1 to 1965:4, and an early version of MPS, Sparks (B13f) also found the average FHA-VA ceiling to be a significant determinant of MSB supply of credit. In this study, he also enters the ceiling rate directly into the starts equation, subject to the condition that it ceases to be an effective constraint when the ratio of ceiling rate to conventional rate reaches the value attained in 1958:3.

VonFurstenberg and Herr (C17) introduce the difference between quarterly levels of secondary market yields on FHA mortgages and the FHA-VA ceiling rate into a starts equation as a credit rationing variable, and find that if the spread were to rise by 100 basis points, starts would decline by 300,000

(SAAR). The authors note, however, that FHA-VA guarantees applied to fewer than 200,000 new units in 1973, and thus that the variable is a proxy for the effects of tightening credit in other sectors as well as in the government sector. Thus, policy action to change the ceiling in accord with changes in the mortgage rate is unlikely to prevent the 300,000 unit decline, although the authors appear to suggest that such action would have that result.

Lin (C8) applies spectral analysis using monthly data and disaggregating starts to the government sector on the one hand and conventional on the other. He finds that starts in the two sectors are cyclically associated with similar variables--monetary base, deposit inflows, and the money supply. In general, availability variables are more important than cost of credit variables. He does find a significant association between the yield differential between FHA and Aa bond yields on the one hand, and FHA/VA starts on the other, which he attributes to the ceilings. However, starts are much less sensitive to this variable than to the monetary base and other credit flow variables.

Like FHA and VA ceilings, usury laws may have the effect of reducing the level of residential construction when the usury ceilings are lower than market rates on alternative investments, if the market does not completely discount the effects of the ceilings. One paper surveyed, Robins (D6), addresses this problem. He uses cross section data from 77 SMSAs in 1970-1971 in two one-equation single-family housing starts models, and finds in his first model that when usury ceilings are below market rates, housing starts are on average approximately 28 percent lower than in SMSAs where the usury ceiling is not effective. In the second model, which allows the difference between the usury limit and the market rate to come into play, Robins finds a 1 percent increase in the usury limit will generate a 16 percent increase in starts. The Robins results are interesting but hardly definitive. The models are essentially ad hoc. There is no construction cost variable, nor other financial variables, and his attempt to incorporate vacancy rates was unsuccessful. Rosen and Kearl (C12) introduce a lagged usury ceiling variable into the mortgage supply equation of their aggregate time series model. The variable is a weighted average of the difference between the market rate and usury ceiling when the market rate is greater than the ceiling, and zero at other times. The variable is insignificant in their 3SLS results reported in the paper, but they report finding a significant negative coefficient in 2SLS estimates. Jaffee (B13g) notes in a footnote (p. 163) that tests to determine whether usury ceilings restrain potential increases in the mortgage rate in the mortgage sector of the MPS model proved insignificant.

A variety of nonstandard mortgage contracts have been proposed to assist housing (see Modigliani and Lessard (F29) for a group of papers on new mortgage designs). Jaffee and Kearl (B13c) simulate a number of these using the housing, mortgage, and savings deposit sectors of the MPS model over the 1962:1 through 1973:4 period. Thirteen simulations were run in addition to the with and without deposit ceiling simulations mentioned above, including: (1) Graduated Payment Mortgages--both fixed graduation and new issue graduation; (2) Variable Rate Mortgages (VRM)--basic short VRM, short-term VRM with deposit rate spread, short-term VRM with reserve constraint, dual-rate VRM with deposit rate spread, and FHLBB VRM with reserve constraint; (3) Constant-Payment-Factor-Variable Rate Mortgage and Price Level Adjusted Mortgage (PLAM). We shall not try to report their results in detail. They describe the results as suggesting that almost all the contracts "could be used without disruption and indeed [would produce] generally beneficial outcomes" (p. 246). It is worth noting that the Jaffee-Kearl exercise is a particularly difficult one to carry out, even with a model with a financial sector as complete as that in the MPS Model. The level of detail is not sufficient to use the model without modification. Accordingly, the authors had to made some essentially ad hoc adjustments in the model, adding variables and equations, and guessing at some parameters. They caution that they cannot claim even the level of precision that might normally be associated with simulation studies.

Finally, Fair and Jaffee simulate several proposals of the President's Commission on Financial Structure and Regulation (the Hunt Commission) to discover effects on mortgages and housing markets. Simulations from this study are cited extensively above. In addition to those already mentioned, Fair and Jaffee simulate extending the service and lending functions of savings institutions, allowing a flexible loan rate on life insurance policy loans, and instituting a variable rate mortgage (VRM). They introduce consumer loan powers and third-party payment functions for S&Ls into the model by assuming relative shifts in the time deposit demand functions of commercial banks and savings institutions. Funds flow to savings institutions, of course. The effect they find on the housing stock is surprisingly strong. Regarding lending functions of savings institutions, they simulate both a portfolio composition effect, accomplished by merely reducing the supply of mortgage lending by S&Ls and MSBs; and a portfolio expansion effect, accomplished by increasing deposit rates which, in turn, stimulate deposit inflows. The net effect of the two on mortgages is either positive or negative, but the effect on the housing stock is always positive. The simulation of a flexible rate for policy loans of life insurance companies was straightforward, since the spread between the fixed rate on policy loans and the market rate is built into the MPS model. The authors find a negligible impact on housing. Finally, the effect of a VRM is introduced by eliminating the lag between the change in the mortgage rate and the change in the deposit rate, since given a VRM, savings institutions can respond more quickly to changing mortgage yields. The particular simulation hardly captures all aspects of VRMs, of course. The result of this simulation is a positive impact on the stock of housing over the simulation period.

V. CONCLUSIONS

The models surveyed here all have their strengths and weaknesses. In particular considerable effort has been applied to modeling the effects of the financial sector on housing starts or investment in residential construction. All models examined contain some financial variables--interest rates, interest rate differentials, mortgage stocks and flows, financial flows into institutions engaged in mortgage lending, FNMA activity, and so on. The degree of sophistication with which financial variables are included varies considerably among the models, of course. The most structurally complete financial sectors appear in the flow of funds models (Bosworth-Duesenberry (B2) and Hendershott (B9)). For example, Bosworth and Duesenberry model separately the three types of nonbank financial intermediaries engaged in mortgage lending activity--S&Ls, mutual savings banks, and life insurance companies--with an equation in each sector (as well as one in the commercial bank sector) to explain changes in mortgage asset holdings. The model contains eleven interest rate equations, including one for the conventional mortgage rate. FHLBB advances are endogenous to the model. In contrast, some major structural models contain an aggregated financial sector with little or no attention to the mortgage sector itself. For example, the Wharton Mark IV model (B18) does not model nonbank financial intermediaries at all. No separate mortgage rate appears in the model. FHLBB advances and FNMA purchases are not included, even exogenously. The financial sector impacts the housing sector through the effect of changes in the gap between long-term interest rates (represented by Moody's Aaa rate) and short-term rates (represented by the 4-6 month prime commercial paper rate).

While many models do not present a formal theoretical separation between a housing services market and a residential construction market, demand variables which can be interpreted in that framework are usually included. Most models contain a price of services variable, although at least one major structural model (DRI (B7)) does not in the version we have reviewed. An income variable is also frequently included, although several models (for example, Fair (B8)) omit it. So-called "basic demand factors"--demographic factors--are left out of most models on grounds that they are not subject to short-run change and thus contribute little to short-run fluctuations being modeled. The Hickman-Coen model (B10), which is an annual model with a relatively long-run orientation, contains the most complete consideration of demographic variables. On the supply side, several models contain an explicit housing stock variable. For example, BEA (B4), MPS (B13), and DRI (B7) all contain equations to calculate the stock. However, many models, for example, Michigan (B14) and Rosen-Kearl (C12), contain no stock variable at all. Operating inputs are rarely considered (but see Chase (B5)). Vacancy rates are particularly emphasized in the work of Maisel (C10) and vacancy equations or variables are contained in other models. For example, in the Wharton model (B18), there are separate equations to explain vacancy rates in owner-occupied and in rental housing units. On the other hand, many models, including some of the major ones (for example, MPS (B13)) do not consider vacancies in their estimating equations.

As for the residential construction sector itself, we have noted that only MPS (B13) and BEA (B4) are cast explicitly in the capital asset pricing framework as we have outlined it. However, many others are basically capital stock adjustment models (for example, Wharton (B18) and DRI (B7)). Most, but not all, models contain some variable to reflect the cost price of housing. The most prominent examples of those that do not are Fair (B8) and Swan (C15). Disaggregation by type of construction is common in the national models (for example, MPS (B13), Brookings (B3), Wharton Annual (B17)), but not in models of the housing sector alone (exceptions include Huang (C5) and Brady (C3)). This disaggregation typically extends only to single- and multifamily units, however. Most models do not include a behavioral equation for mobile homes (DRI (B7) and Chase (B5) contain mobile home equations) or for additions and alterations (exceptions include Chase (B5) and Wharton Annual (B17)).

The strengths of some models are the weaknesses of others. For example, the Bosworth-Duesenberry model (B2), which has a highly disaggregated financial sector, contains a single equation in the residential construction sector. That equation does little more than translate changes in the mortgage stock, derived from the detailed financial side model, into changes in investment in residential construction. The model also contains a vacancy equation which has no direct impact on the residential construction equation.

The weakness common to nearly all models surveyed is the lack of detail in the construction inputs sector. Most housing sector models contain only an exogenous construction costs index, usually the Boeckh index. A few (for example, McDonough (C9)) contain labor and materials costs directly. The national models often determine the cost price endogenously, but without detailed construction inputs independent variables. For example, in the MPS model (B13), the construction cost index is derived by assuming a fixed ratio between the endogenous price deflator for nonfarm business production and construction costs. It is in the construction inputs sector where there is most glaring need for further modeling effort. Policies directed at that sector cannot be adequately analyzed with current models.

An additional issue, noted earlier, relates to the strengths and weaknesses of the models. Models of the housing sector per se are inherently weaker theoretically than full structural models because housing sector models cannot allow for the full set of interactions with the rest of the economy. Exclusive reliance on a model (or models) of the housing sector is, then, likely at some point to provide misleading results. Further, one of the major benefits of simulation is that the exercise reveals very subtle dynamic feedbacks which would otherwise remain obscured. Even if the quantitative results from a simulation are suspect, a researcher made aware of the feedbacks can analyze their importance, outside the context of the model. A model of the housing sector exclusively, by truncating the feedbacks, is in a sense less useful as a result. On the other hand, increasing the size, and thus the complexity, of a model necessarily increases the danger of misspecification and the results of simulations using full structural models may be no more reliable than those using a simple housing sector model. There is, in fact, a considerable large vs. small model controversy in the model literature. Thus, despite the inability to allow for feedbacks from the other sectors, structural models of the housing sector alone should not be ignored in policy analysis.

Aside from considerations of the general structural detail of a model, there is the question of the policy variables per se. As we have noted, a given policy cannot be analyzed unless the model contains a variable which is a reasonable proxy for the policy. In many cases, as we have seen, the policy is not explicitly represented. Deciding on an appropriate policy proxy is a severe test of a model user's ingenuity and expertise. Familiarity with the model being used is crucial, and it is worth noting that most of the simulations reported above are the work of the authors of the models. Appropriate policy proxies do not always exist, of course, regardless of the user's ingenuity. For example, one cannot simulate a mortgage market policy with the Michigan model (B14) because the model contains no mortgage sector at all. The lack of specific policy variables, while frustrating to those who wish to test the effects of changing selected policies, is not surprising, given that the main purpose of most of the models is to analyze short cycles--either of the housing sector or of the economy in general. Policy variables which are not often changed--for example, the deductibility provisions under the income tax of mortgage interest and property tax payments, do not commonly appear in the models since they have little influence on short-run fluctuations. There are exceptions. The Wharton model (B18) appears to have more potential than others for analysis of tax provisions in that the tax and transfer section of the model contains disaggregation of tax payments by income class and provides estimating equations for federal tax deductions, exemptions, and state and local property taxes. No tax features are built directly into the housing sector equations, however. Policy flow variables subject to frequent change, such as FNMA acquisitions, are much more commonly introduced. The alternative to choosing a policy proxy is to respecify the model, adding variables and equations which more precisely represent the policy of interest. Such additions, which are likely to be somewhat ad hoc, present a danger of misspecification, particularly for the large models. In addition, reestimation, if that is to be done, is in itself a formidable task.

The model which has been used for the widest range of published policy simulations is the MPS model (B13). It is reasonably well "balanced" and in structural conformance with the theory we have described above. Exclusive reliance on the MPS model is not to be recommended, however. The financial sector of the model in general, and the mortgage sector in particular, while more detailed than in most of the models surveyed, lacks the rich detail of the financial sectors of the flow of funds models (Bosworth-Duesenbery (B2) and Hendershott (B9)). Financing is regarded by most analysts as crucial to explaining short-run fluctuations. The real sector of the MPS model, while more detailed than in many models, lacks the detail of, for example, the Wharton models (B17 and B18). Moreover, the multifamily sector of the MPS model, in particular, is not completely satisfactory (see B13d).

In sum, the conclusion that emerges most clearly is that no one model among those surveyed is best for policy analysis of the housing sector. Our point is not to condemn models for what they do not do, but rather to emphasize that no one model does, or is intended to do, everything. For example, if the long-run (say 10 to 20 years) effects of a particular policy are to be considered, demographic factors should not be ignored, as they are, and reasonably so, in quarterly models. If a policy affecting one segment of the financial sector, say S&Ls, is to be considered, a far more complete analysis can be done using a model which disaggregates in the financial sector. On the other hand, the model with a detailed financial sector tends to have a relatively rudimentary real sector. Confidence in one's analysis, then, necessitates the use of a variety of models. Models which aggregate on the financial side miss important determinants of residential construction, but models which aggregate on the real side also miss important determinants. Thus, the results from one model alone are likely to be misleading. Edwards (A1), in effect, does what we are advocating here by bringing together results from 12 different models regarding the impact of FHLBB advances. It is reasonable, in our opinion, to conclude based on his work that FHLBB advances have significant short-run effects. This consensus of the models exists even though the 12 differ widely in specification and data employed. Further confidence in one's analysis may be gained by estimating and simulating the models using the same data over similar time periods. Edwards reports some efforts in this direction. See also Grebler and Maisel (A5).

Finally, even if the state of econometric modeling of the housing sector were far more advanced, it is well to note that

> [no] econometric model is any more than a tentative statement about the economy's interactive logic and it can never contain any more information than was fed into it in the process of construction. In many forecasting and policy uses this information is simply inadequate, and in some cases new events impinge on the economy which--even if only temporarily--break the logic which has been deduced from past events. Even if we had a model whose every error statistic was at least 50 percent less than those [we have found], it would still take an economist who watches what goes on in the economy to communicate with the model and make sensible use of it for real-time forecasting and policy purposes. (B14b, pp. 652-653.)

BIBLIOGRAPHY

The bibliography is organized into seven sections: Surveys, National Economic Models, National Housing Models, Other Housing Models, Foreign Models, Related Work, and Data Sources. The presentation is alphabetical except that papers relating to a particular model are grouped in one place. For example, under the MPS model are listed seven papers by several different authors.

The literature search was largely confined to published material. No systematic attempt was made to collect unpublished material, although some unpublished material was examined. Unpublished sources are cited below when the material is generally available.

A. Surveys

1. Edwards, Donald G. "The Effects of FHLBB Advances on Housing Starts and Mortgage Flows: A Summary of Selected Empirical Studies" Federal Home Loan Bank Board, Office of Economic Research Working Paper #60, November 1975.

2. Fair, Ray C. "Disequilibrium in Housing Models" Journal of Finance, Papers and Proceedings, May 1972, Vol. 27, pp. 207-221.

3. Fromm, Gary "Econometric Models of the Residential Construction Sector: A Comparison" in R. Bruce Ricks, ed. National Housing Models Lexington Mass: Heath Lexington, 1973, pp. 125-155.

4. Geisel, M. "A Survey of Time Series and Cross-Section Studies of Housing" unpublished, Carnegie-Mellon University, 1971.

5. Grebler, Leo, and Maisel, Sherman J. "Determinants of Residential Construction: A Review of Present Knowledge" in D. B. Suits, Robert Eisner, and R. H. Strotz Impacts of Monetary Policy, Englewood Cliffs: Prentice Hall Inc. 1963, pp. 475-620.

6. Kalchbrenner, J. H. "Theoretical and Empirical Specifications of the Housing Sector," in Federal Reserve Staff Study, Ways to Moderate Fluctuations in Housing Constructions, Washington: Board of Governors of the Federal Reserve System, December 1972, pp. 253-274.

7. Kearl, James, Rosen K. and Swan C. "Relationships between the Mortgage Instruments, the Demand for Housing, and Mortgage Credit: A Review of Empirical Studies" in Franco Modigliani and Donald Lessard, eds. New Mortgage Designs for Stable Housing in an Inflationary Environment, Federal Reserve Bank of Boston Conference Series No. 14, 1975.

7a. Kearl, Rosen and Swan "The Financial Determinants of the Demand for Housing" Massachusetts Institute of Technology, Sloan School of Management Working Paper No. 796-75, January 1975.

B.   National Economic Models

The housing sector embedded in a national model is often the subject of an individual paper or chapter in a book describing the entire model. Sometimes, however, there is no published discussion of the housing equations alone. Further, models undergo major changes in structure over time that render early discussions out of date. Each of the papers cited below contains the housing sector equations of a national model at some stage of the development of the model. In some cases, there is no explicit discussion of that sector at all, and in others, the discussion is brief. In addition to the sources cited below, unpublished materials relating to more current versions of the following models were surveyed: BEA, Chase, MPS, Michigan, Wharton Annual, and Wharton Mark IV.

1.   Bloch, B. W. and Pilgrim, J. D. "A Reappraisal of Some Factors Associated with the Fluctuations in the United States in the Interwar Period" Southern Economic Journal, January 1973, Vol. 39, No. 3, pp. 327-344.

2.   Bosworth-Duesenberry Model

     2a. Bosworth, Barry and Duesenberry, J. S. "A Flow of Funds Model and its Implications" Issues in Federal Debt Management, Federal Reserve Bank of Boston Conference Series No. 10, June 1973.

     2b. Duesenberry, J. S. and Bosworth, Barry "Policy Implications of a Flow-of-Funds Model" Journal of Finance, May 1974, Vol. 29, No. 2, pp. 331-347.

3.   Brookings Model

     3a. Maisel, Sherman J. "Nonbusiness Construction" in J. S. Duesenberry, G. Fromm, L.R. Klein and E. Kuh, eds. The Brookings Quarterly Econometric Model of the United States, Skokie, Ill: Rand McNally and Co., 1965, pp. 180-201.

     3b. Fromm, Gary and Taubman, Paul Policy Simulations With an Econometric Model, Washington: The Brookings Institution, 1968.

     3c. Fromm, Gary, Klein, L. R. and Schink, G. R. "Short and Long-Term Simulations with the Brookings Model" in Bert G. Hickman, ed. Econometric Models of Cyclical Behavior, Studies in Income and Wealth, Vol. 1, No. 36, New York: National Bureau of Economic Research, 1972, pp. 201-300.

3d. Schink, George R. "An Evaluation of the Predictive Abilities of a Large Model: Post-Sample Simulations with the Brookings Model" in G. Fromm and L. Klein, eds. <u>The Brookings Model: Perspective and Recent Developments</u>, Amsterdam: North Holland Publishing Co., 1975, pp. 259-351.

4. Bureau of Economic Analysis Model (BEA)

4a. Green, George R., Liebenberg, M. and Hirsch, A. A. "Short and Long-Term Simulations with the OBE Econometric Model" in B.G. Hickman, ed. <u>Econometric Models of Cyclical Behavior</u>, Studies in Income and Wealth, Vol. 1, No. 36, New York: National Bureau of Economic Research, 1972, pp. 25-138.

4b. Hirsch, Albert A., Liebenberg, Maurice and Green, G. R. <u>The BEA Quarterly Econometric Model</u>, BEA Staff paper No. 22, U.S. Department of Commerce, Bureau of Economic Analysis, July 1973, pp. 21-31.

5. Chase Econometrics Model

6. Chow, Gregory C. and Moore, Goeffrey H. "An Econometric Model of Business Cycles" in Bert G. Hickman, ed. <u>Econometric Models of Cyclical Behavior</u>, Studies in Income and Wealth, Vol. 2, No. 36, New York: National Bureau of Economic Research, 1972, pp. 739-809.

7. Data Resources Inc. Model (DRI)

7a. Eckstein, Otto, Green, E. W. and Sinai, A. "The Data Resources Model: Uses, Structure and Analysis of the U.S. Economy" <u>International Economic Review</u>, October 1974, Vol. 15, No. 3., pp. 595-615.

7b. Fromm, Gary and Sinai, Allen "A Policy Simulation of Deposit Flows, Mortgage Sector Activity, and Housing" Paper presented at the Econometric Society Meeting, December 1974.

8. Fair Model

8a. Fair, Ray C. <u>A Short-Run Forecasting Model of the United States Economy</u>, Lexington, Mass: Heath Lexington, 1971.

8b. Fair, Ray C. "Monthly Housing Starts" in R. Bruce Ricks, ed. <u>National Housing Models</u>, Lexington Mass: Heath Lexington, 1973, pp. 69-92.

8c. Fair, Ray C. and Jaffee, D. M. "Methods of Estimation for Markets in Disequilibrium" <u>Econometrica</u>, May 1972, Vol. 40, No. 3, pp. 497-514.

8d. Fair, Ray C. and Kelejian, H. H. "Methods of Estimation for Markets in Disequilibrium: A Further Study" _Econometrica_, January 1974, Vol. 42, No. 1, pp. 177-190.

9. Hendershott Model

9a. Hendershott, Patrick _A Flow-of-Funds Financial Model: Estimation and Applications to Financial Policies and Reforms_, Lexington, Mass: Heath Lexington, 1977.

9b. Hendershott, Patrick H. and Villani, Kevin E. "The Federally Sponsored Credit Agencies: Their Behavior and Impact" Paper presented at the Meeting of the Econometric Society, San Francisco, December 1974. Revised Version, January 1977.

10. Hickman-Coen Model

10a. Hickman, Bert G. "What Became of the Building Cycle?" in P. A. David and M. W. Reder, eds. _Nations and Households in Economic Growth_, New York: Academic Press, 1974.

10b. Hickman, Bert G. and Coen, Robert M. _An Annual Growth Model of the U.S. Economy_, Contributions to Economic Analysis, No. 100, New York: American Elsevier; Amsterdam and Oxford: North-Holland, 1976.

11. Liu, T. C. "An Explanatory Quarterly Econometric Model of Effective Demand in the Postwar U.S. Economy" _Econometrica_, July 1963, Vol. 41, No. 3, pp. 301-348.

12. Liu, T. C. and Hwa, E. C. "A Monthly Econometric Model of the U.S. Economy" _International Economic Review_, June 1974, Vol. 15, No. 2, pp. 328-365.

13. MIT-Pennsylvania-SSRC (MPS) Model

13a. de Leeuw, Frank and Gramlich, E. M. "The Channels of Monetary Policy" _Federal Reserve Bulletin_, June 1969, Vol. 55, No. 6, pp. 472-491.

13b. Fair, Ray C. and Jaffee, D. M. "Implications of the Proposals of the Hunt Commission for the Mortgage and Housing Markets: An Empirical Study" _Policies for a More Competitive Financial System_, Federal Reserve Bank of Boston Conference Series No. 8, 1972.

13c. Jaffee, Dwight M. and Kearl, James R. "Macroeconomic Simulations of Alternative Mortgage Instruments" in F. Modigliani and D. Lessard, eds. _New Mortgage Designs for Stable Housing in an Inflationary Environment_, Federal Reserve Bank of Boston Conference Series No. 14, January 1975, pp. 211-254.

13d. Kalchbrenner, John H. "A Model of the Housing Sector" in E. M. Gramlich and D. M. Jaffee, eds. <u>Savings Deposits, Mortgages and Housing</u>, Lexington Mass.: Heath Lexington, 1972.

13e. Kalchbrenner, John H. "A Summary of the Current Financial Intermediary, Mortgage, and Housing Sectors of the FRB-MIT-Penn Econometric Model" in R. Bruce Ricks, ed. <u>National Housing Models</u>, Lexington Mass.: Heath Lexington, 1973, pp. 93-124.

13f. Sparks, Gordon R. "A Model of the Mortgage Market and Residential Construction Activity" <u>1967 Proceedings of the Business and Economic Statistics Section</u>, Washington: American Statistical Association, 1967, pp. 77-85.

13g. Jaffee, Dwight M. "An Econometric Model of the Mortgage Market" in E. M. Gramlich and D. M. Jaffee, eds. <u>Savings Deposits, Mortgages and Housing</u>, Lexington Mass: Heath Lexington, 1972, pp. 139-209.

14. Michigan Model

14a. Hymans, Saul H. and H. T. Shapiro <u>The DHL-III Quarterly Econometric Model of the U.S. Economy</u>, Research Seminar in Quantitative Economics University of Michigan, 1970.

14b. Hymans, Saul H. and H. T. Shapiro "The Structure and Properties of the Michigan Quarterly Econometric Model of the U.S. Economy" <u>International Economic Review</u>, October 1974, Vol. 15, No. 3, October 1974, pp. 632-653.

15. Silber, William L. <u>Portfolio Behavior of Financial Institutions</u>, New York: Holt, Rinehart and Winston, 1970.

16. Suits, Daniel B. "Forecasting and Analysis with an Econometric Model" <u>American Economic Review</u>, March 1962, Vol. 52, No. 1, pp. 104-132.

17. The Wharton Annual and Industry Model

18. Wharton Quarterly Model

18a. Evans, Michael K. <u>Macroeconomic Activity</u>, New York: Harper and Row, 1969, Chapter 7, pp. 184-200.

18b. McCarthy, M. D. <u>The Wharton Quarterly Econometric Forecasting Model, Mark III</u>, Studies in Quantitative Economics No. 6, Wharton School of Finance and Commerce, 1972.

C. <u>National Housing Models</u>

The papers cited below present aggregated national time series models of the U.S. housing sector. Each study contains at least one housing starts or housing expenditures equation, although the author's primary purpose in some cases is to model the mortgage market and not the market for residential construction.

1. Arcelus, F. and Meltzer, A. "The Market for Housing and Housing Services" <u>Journal of Money, Credit and Banking</u>, January 1973, Vol. 5, No. 1, pp. 78-99.

    1a. Swan, Craig "The Markets for Housing and Housing Services" <u>Journal of Money Credit, and Banking</u>, November 1973, Vol. 5, No. 4, pp. 960-972.

    1b. Arcelus, F. and Meltzer, A. "Reply" <u>Journal of Money, Credit and Banking</u>, November 1973, Vol. 5, No. 4, pp. 973-978.

2. Brady, Eugene A. "A Sectoral Econometric Study of the Postwar Residential Housing Market" <u>Journal of Political Economy</u>, April 1967, Vol. 75, No. 2, pp. 147-158.

    2a. Smith, L. B. "A Sectoral Econometric Study of the Postwar Residential Housing Market: An Opposite View" <u>Journal of Political Economy</u>, March-April 1970, Vol. 78, No. 2, pp. 268-273.

    2b. Brady, E. A. "A Sectoral Econometric Study of the Postwar Residential Housing Market: An Opposite View: Reply" <u>Journal of Political Economy</u>, March-April 1970, Vol. 78, No. 2, pp. 274-278.

3. Brady, Eugene A. "An Econometric Analysis of the U.S. Residential Housing Market" in R. Bruce Ricks, ed. <u>National Housing Models</u>, Lexington Mass: Heath Lexington, 1973, pp. 1-47.

4. Cassidy, H.J. and Valentini, J. "A Quarterly Econometric Model of the U.S. Housing, Mortgage, and Deposit Markets" unpublished, 1972 Winter meetings of the American Real Estate and Urban Economics Association.

5. Huang, D. S. "A Study of the Market for New Housing Units," <u>1969 Proceedings of the Business and Economic Section</u>, Washington: American Statistical Association, 1969, pp. 702-711.

6. Huang, David S. "Effect of Different Credit Policies on Housing Demand" in Irwin Friend, Dir. <u>Study of the Savings and Loan Industry</u>, Washington: Federal Home Loan Bank Board, July 1969, pp. 1211-1239.

7. Lee, T. H. "The Stock Demand Elasticities of Nonfarm Housing" _Review of Economics and Statistics_, February 1964, Vol. 46, No. 1, pp. 82–89.

8. Lin, Steven A. Y. "Effects of Monetary Policy and Credit Conditions on the Housing Sector" _American Real Estate and Urban Economics Association Journal_, June 1973, Vol. 1, pp. 8–30.

9. McDonough, William R. "Buyers, Builders, and Instability in Single-Family Housing Construction" _Journal of Economics and Business_, Winter 1975, Vol. 27., No. 3, pp. 150–158.

10. Maisel Model

    10a. Maisel, Sherman J.   "A Theory of Fluctuations in Residential Construction Starts" _American Economic Review_, June 1963, Vol. 53, No. 3, pp. 359–383.

    10b. Maisel, Sherman J. "The Effects of Monetary Policy on Expenditures in Specific Sectors of the Economy" _Journal of Political Economy_, July–August 1968, Vol. 76, No. 4, Pt. II, pp. 796–814.

    10c. Burnham, James B. "Housing Starts in 1966 and 1969: A Comparison Using an Econometric Model" in R. Bruce Ricks, ed. _National Housing Models_, Lexington Mass: Heath Lexington, 1973, pp. 49–67.

    10d. Burnham, James B. "Housing Starts in 1966 and 1969: A Comparison Using an Econometric Model" _Land Economics_, February 1972, Vol. 48, No. 1, pp. 88–89.

11. Muth, R. F. "The Demand for Nonfarm Housing" in A. C. Harberger, ed. _The Demand for Durable Goods_, Chicago: University of Chicago Press, 1960.

12. Rosen, K. T. and Kearl, J. R. "A Model of Housing Starts, Mortgage Flows, and the Behavior of the Federal Home Loan Bank Board and the Federal National Mortgage Association" Harvard–MIT Joint Center for Urban Studies Working Paper No. 27, May 1974.

13. Sparks, Gordon "An Econometric Analysis of the Role of Financial Intermediaries in Postwar Residential Building Cycles" in Robert Ferber, ed. _Determinants of Investment Behavior_, New York: National Bureau of Economic Research, 1967, pp. 301–331.

14. Swan, Craig "Homebuilding: A Review of Experience" _Brookings Papers on Economic Activity_, 1:1970, pp. 48–76.

15. Swan Model

    15a. Swan, Craig "A Quarterly Model of Housing Starts: A Disequilibrium Approach" Federal Home Loan Bank Board Working Paper No. 39, 1972.

15b. Swan, Craig "Housing Subsidies and Housing Starts" <u>American Real Estate and Urban Economics Association Journal</u>, Fall 1973, Vol. 1, pp. 119-140.

16. Utt, Ronald "An Empirical Analysis of the GNMA Tandem Plan" in Robert M. Buckley, John A. Tuccilo, and Kevin E. Villani, eds. <u>Capital Markets and The Housing Sector: Perspectives on Financial Reform</u>, Cambridge Mass: Ballinger Publishing Co., 1977, pp. 347-362.

17. vonFurstenberg, George M. and Herr, Eric B. "The Normal Demand for Housing Completions and the Stock Adjustment Process in Housing Starts" <u>Journal of Economics and Business</u>, Winter 1975, Vol. 27, No. 2, pp. 131-140.

D. Other Housing Sector Models

The models listed below all contain at least one housing starts or housing expenditure equation. Included are studies using cross section data or subnational time series data, and papers which examine a particular aspect of the housing sector, rather than modeling that sector completely.

1. Fair, Ray C. "Application of a Housing Model to SMSA Data" Federal Home Loan Bank Board Invited Working Paper No. 4, June 1972.

2. Huang, D. S. "Short-Run Instability in Single-Family Housing Starts" <u>Journal of the American Statistical Association</u>, December 1973, Vol. 68, No. 344, pp. 788-792.

3. Kartman, Arthur E. "Demand for Housing: The Neglected Supply Side" <u>University of Washington Business Review</u>, Spring 1971, Vol. 31, No. 1, pp. 59-64.

4. Krekorian, G. P. "The Demand for Residential Construction-Pomona, California" <u>American Economist</u>, Fall 1972, Vol. 16, No. 2, pp. 4-16.

5. Pollock, R. "Supply of Residential Construction: A Cross Section Examination of Recent Housing Market Behavior" <u>Land Economics</u>, February 1973, Vol. 49, No. 1, pp. 57-66.

6. Robins, Philip K. "The Effects of State Usury Ceilings on Single Family Homebuilding" <u>Journal of Finance</u>, March 1974, Vol. 29, No. 1, pp. 227-235.

7. Taubman, Paul, and Rasche, Robert "Tax Laws and the Apartment Building Industry" unpublished, University of Pennsylvania, 1971.

8. Winger, Alan R. "Short-Term Activity in Residential Construction Markets: Some Regional Considerations" <u>Southern Economic Journal</u>, April 1970, Vol. 36, No. 4, pp. 390-403.

9. Winger, Alan R. "Short Term Fluctuations in Residential Construction: An Overview of Recent Research" <u>Mississippi Valley Journal of Business and Economics</u>, Spring 1970, Vol. 5, No. 3, pp. 31-51.

10. Winger, Alan R. "Residential Construction, Acceleration, and Urban Growth" <u>Journal of Regional Science</u>, April 1971, Vol. 11, No. 1, pp. 91-100.

11. Winger, Alan R. "Demand and Residential Fluctuations" <u>Nebraska Journal of Economics and Business</u>, Summer 1971, Vol. 10, No. 3, pp. 51-61.

E. <u>Foreign Models</u>

Below is a selected list of papers presenting foreign housing models. Several of those listed are frequently referenced in the U.S. literature.

1. Bebee, E. L. "Regional Housing Markets and Population Flows in Canada 1956-67" <u>Canadian Journal of Economics</u>, August 1972, Vol. 5, No. 3, pp. 386-397.

2. Chung, Joseph H. <u>Cyclical Instability in Residential Construction in Canada</u>, Ottawa: Economic Council of Canada, 1976.

3. Hamdani, D. H. "Interprovincial Differences in the Behavior of Housing Starts in Canada" <u>Revista Internazionale di Scienze Economiche e Commerciale</u>, September 1975, Vol. 22, No. 9, pp. 893-911.

4. Nobay A. R. "Short Term Forecasting of Housing Investment - A Note" <u>National Institute Economic Review</u>, August 1967, No. 41.

5. Smith, Lawrence B. <u>The Postwar Canadian Housing and Residential Mortgage Markets and the Role of Government</u>, Buffalo and Toronto: University of Toronto Press, 1974.

6. Smith, Lawrence B. <u>Housing and Mortgage Markets in Canada</u>, Bank of Canada Staff Research Studies No. 6, Ottawa: Publications Committee, Bank of Canada, 1970.

7. Smith, Lawrence B. "A Model of the Canadian housing and Mortgage Markets" <u>Journal of Political Economy</u>, September-October 1969, Vol. 77, No. 5, pp. 795-816.

8. Smith, Lawrence B. "A Bi-Sectoral Housing Market Model" <u>Canadian Journal of Economics</u>, November 1969, Vol. 2, No. 4, pp. 557-569.

9. Whitehead, C. M. "A Model of the UK Housing Market" <u>Bulletin of the Oxford University Institute of Economics and Statistics</u>, November 1971, Vol. 33, No. 4, pp. 245-266.

F.   Related Work

The papers listed below do not contain housing starts or housing expenditures equations, but are nonetheless of interest to researchers interested
in housing models. Included are econometric mortgage market models
(Clauretie), analyses of "long cycles" (Campbell), selected studies of
housing demand (deLeeuw), books from which are drawn several items appearing
elsewhere in the bibliography, and other items referenced in the text.

1.   Alberts, William W.   "Business Cycles, Residential Construction
     Cycles and the Mortgage Market" Journal of Political Economy, June
     1962, Vol. 70, No. 3, pp. 263-281.

2.   Atkinson, L. J.   "Long-term Influences Affecting the Volume of New
     Housing Units" Survey of Current Business, November 1963, Vol. 43,
     No. 11, pp. 8-19.

3.   Ball, Robert, and Ludwig, L.   "Labor Requirements for Construction
     of Single-Family Houses" Monthly Labor Review, September 1971, Vol.
     94, No. 9.

4.   Brady, Eugene A.   "Regional Cycles in Residential Construction
     and the Interregional Mortgage Market: 1954-1959" Land Economics,
     February 1963, Vol. 39, No. 1, pp. 15-30.

5.   Campbell, Burnham O.   Population Change and Building Cycles, Bureau
     of Economic and Business Research at the University of Illinois
     Bulletin No. 91, Urbana, Ill.,1966.

     5a.   Campbell, B. O. "Long Swings in Residential Construction: The
           Postwar Experience" American Economic Review, May 1963, Vol.
           53, No. 2, pp. 508-518.

6.   Cargill, T. F.   "Construction Activity and Secular Change in the
     United States" Applied Economics, June 1971, Vol. 3, No. 2, pp.
     85-97.

7.   Cochran, D. and Orcutt, G.   "Sampling Study of the Merits of Auto-
     regressive and Reduced Form Transmissions in Regression Analysis"
     Journal of the American Statistical Association, 1949, Vol. 44, pp.
     356-372.

8.   Clauretie, T. M.   "Interest Rates, the Business Demand for Funds,
     and the Residential Mortgage Market: A Sectoral Econometric Study"
     Journal of Finance, December 1973, Vol. 28, No. 5, pp. 1313-1326.

9.   Clauretie, T. M.   "Interest Rates and the Sectoral Behavior of the
     Residential Mortgage Market: A Theoretical Model" Southern Economic
     Journal, July 1974, Vol. 41, No. 1, pp. 103-108.

10. de Leeuw, Frank   "The Demand for Housing: A Review of Cross-Section
     Evidence" Review of Economics and Statistics, February 1971, Vol.
     53, No. 1, pp. 1-10.

10a. Maisel, S. J., Burnham, J. B. and Austin, S. S. "The Demand for Housing: Comment" Review of Economics and Statistics, November 1971, Vol. 53, No. 4, pp. 410-413.

11. de Leeuw, F. and Ekanem, N. F. "The Supply of Rental Housing" American Economic Review, December 1971, Vol. 61, No. 5, pp. 806-817.

12. deLeeuw, Frank, and Struyk, Raymond J. The Web of Urban Housing, Washington, D.C.: The Urban Institute, 1975.

13. Dunlop, John, and Mills, Daniel "Manpower in Construction" The Report of the President's Committee on Urban Housing, Washington, D.C., 1968.

14. Easterlin, R. A. "Economic-Demographic Interactions and Long Swings in the Rate of Growth" American Economic Review, December 1966, Vol.56, No. 5, pp. 1063-1104.

15. Federal Reserve Bank of Boston, Housing and Monetary Policy, Conference Series No. 4, October 1970.

16. Federal Reserve Bank of Boston, Policies for a More Competitive Financial System, Conference Series No. 8, 1972.

17. Federal Reserve Staff Study: Ways to Moderate Fluctuations in Housing Construction, Washington: Board of Governors of the Federal Reserve System, December 1972.

18. Fishman, G. S. Spectral Methods in Econometrics, Cambridge: Harvard University Press, 1969.

19. Friend, Irwin (Director) Study of the Savings and Loan Industry, 4 Vols., prepared for the Federal Home Loan Bank Board, Washington, D.C., July 1969.

20. Fromm, Gary, and L. R. Klein (eds.) The Brookings Model: Perspective and Recent Developments, Amsterdam: North Holland Publishing Co., 1975.

21. Gibson, W. E. "Protecting Homebuilding from Restrictive Credit Conditions" Brookings Papers Economic Activity, 1973:3, pp. 647-691.

22. Gramley, Lyle E. "Short-Term Cycles in Housing Production: An Overview of the Problem and Possible Solutions" Federal Reserve Staff Study: Ways to Moderate Fluctuations in Housing Construction, Washington: Board of Governors of the Federal Reserve System, December 1972, pp. 1-67.

23. Gramlich, Edward M. and Jaffee, D. M. (eds.) Savings Deposits, Mortgages and Housing, Lexington, Mass: Heath Lexington, 1972.

24. Granger, C. W. J., and Hatanaka, M. Spectral Analysis in Economic Time Series, Princeton: Princeton University Press, 1964.

25. Guttentag, J. M. "The Short Cycle in Residential Construction, 1946-1959" American Economic Review, June 1961, Vol. 51, No. 3, pp. 275-298.

26. Hickman, Bert G. (ed.) Econometric Models of Cyclical Behavior, 2 Vols., Studies in Income and Wealth No. 36, New York: National Bureau of Economic Research, 1972.

27. Hildreth, Clifford, and Lu, J. Y. "Demand Relations with Auto-correlated Disturbances" Michigan State University, Agricultural Experiment Station Technical Bulletin 276, November 1960.

28. Huang, Davis S. "The Short-term Flows of Nonfarm Residential Mortgages" Econometrica, April 1966, Vol. 34, No. 2, pp. 433-459.

29. Huang, David S. and McCarthy, M. D. "Simulation of the Home Mortgage Market in the Late Sixties" Review of Economics and Statistics, November 1967, Vol. 69, No. 4, pp. 441-450.

30. Jaffee, Dwight M. "The Impact of Removing Regulation Q Ceilings from Savings and Loan Associations" Journal of the Federal Home Loan Bank Board, August 1973.

31. Marcin, Thomas C. Projections of Demand for Housing by Type of Unit and Region, U.S. Department of Agriculture Forest Service, Agriculture Handbook No. 428, May 1972.

    31a. Marcin, Thomas C. The Effects of Declining Population Growth on the Demand for Housing, U.S. Department of Agriculture Forest Service, General Technical Report No. 11, 1974.

32. Meltzer, Allan H. "Credit Availability and Economic Decisions: Some Evidence from the Mortgage and Housing Markets" Journal of Finance, June 1974, Vol. 29, No. 3, pp. 763-777.

33. Modigliani, Franco, and Lessard, Donald R. (eds.) New Mortgage Designs for Stable Housing in an Inflationary Environment, Federal Reserve Bank of Boston Conference Series No. 14, January 1975.

34. Muth, Richard "Interest Rates, Contract Terms and the Allocation of Mortgage Funds" Journal of Finance, March 1962, Vol. 17, No. 1, pp. 63-80.

35. Muth, Richard F. Cities and Housing, Chicago: University of Chicago Press, 1968.

36. Paldam, M. "What is Known about the Housing Demand?" Swedish Economic Journal, June 1970, Vol. 64, No. 4, pp. 124-137.

37. Polinsky, A. Mitchell "The Demand for Housing: A Study in Specification and Grouping" Econometrica, March 1977, Vol. 45, No. 2, pp. 447-461.

38. Reid, Margaret Housing and Income, Chicago: University of Chicago Press, 1962.

39. Ricks, R. Bruce (ed.) National Housing Models. Application of Econometric Techniques to Problems of Housing Research, Proceedings of a Conference Sponsored by the Federal Home Loan Bank System. Studies in Business, Technology, and Economics, Lexington Mass.; Toronto and London: D.C. Heath, 1973.

40. Silber, W. L. "A Model of Federal Home Loan Bank System and Federal National Mortgage Association Behavior" Review of Economics and Statistics, August 1973, Vol. 55, No. 3, pp. 308-320.

41. Stern, A. "Fluctuations in Residential Construction: Some Evidence from the Spectral Estimates" Review of Economics and Statistics, August 1972, Vol. 54, No. 3, pp. 328-332.

42. Swan, Craig "Labor and Material Requirements for Housing" Brookings Papers on Economic Activity, 1971:2, pp. 347-377.

43. Swan, Craig "A General Equilibrium Model of FHLB and FNMA Actions" Federal Home Loan Bank Board Office of Economic Research Working Paper No. 44, July 1973.

44. Taubman, Paul, and Rasche, R. H. "Economic and Tax Depreciation of Office Buildings" National Tax Journal, September 1969, Vol. 22, No. 3.

45. Winger, A. R. "Interarea Variations in Vacancy Rates" Land Economics, February 1967, Vol. 43, No. 1, pp. 84-90.

G. Data

a. Bureau of the Census

1. U.S. Bureau of Census, 1972 Census of Construction Industries.

2. U.S. Bureau of the Census, Census of Housing 1970 (Census of Housing also taken for 1940, 50, 60).

3. U.S. Bureau of the Census, Census of Population 1970.

4. U.S. Bureau of the Census, Historical Statistics of the United States, Colonial Times to 1970.

5. U.S. Bureau of the Census, 1956 National Housing Inventory, 1958.

6. U.S. Bureau of the Census, Housing Construction Statistics, 1889 to 1964, 1966.

7. U.S. Bureau of the Census, New One-Family Homes Sold and For Sale, 1963 to 1967, 1969.

8. U.S. Bureau of the Census, New One-Family Homes Contractor Built 1963 to 1967, 1969.

9. U.S. Bureau of the Census, Housing Starts 1959 to 1971, 1972.

10. U.S. Bureau of the Census, Current Construction Reports Series C-20 "Housing Starts" (monthly).

11. U.S. Bureau of the Census, Current Construction Reports Series C-21 "New Residential Construction in Selected Metropolitan Statistical Areas" (quarterly).

12. U.S. Bureau of the Census, Current Construction Reports Series C-22 "Housing Completions" (monthly).

13. U.S. Bureau of the Census, Current Construction Reports Series C-25 "New One-Family Houses Sold and For Sale" (monthly and annual).

14. U.S. Bureau of the Census, Current Construction Report Series C-27 "Price Index of New One-Family Houses Sold" (quarterly).

15. U.S. Bureau of the Census, Current Construction Reports Series C-30 "Value of New Construction Put in Place" (monthly).

16. U.S. Bureau of the Census, Current Construction Reports Series C-40 "Housing Authorized by Building Permits and Public Contracts" (monthly and annual).

17. U.S. Bureau of the Census, Current Construction Reports Series C-41 "Authorized Construction - Washington, D.C." (monthly).

18. U.S. Bureau of the Census, Current Construction Reports Series C-45 "Housing Units Authorized for Demolition in Permit-Issuing Places" (annual).

19. U.S. Bureau of the Census, Current Construction Reports Series C-50 "Residential Alterations and Repairs" (quarterly [quarterly to be discontinued] and annual).

20. U.S. Bureau of the Census, Current Housing Reports Series H-111 "Vacant Housing Units in the United States" (quarterly and annual) (annual report title "Vacancy Rates and Characteristics of Housing in the United States").

21. U.S. Bureau of the Census, Current Housing Reports Series H-130 "Market Absorption of Apartments" (quarterly and annual).

22. U.S. Bureau of the Census, Current Housing Reports Series H-131 "Characteristics of Apartments Completed" (annual).

23. U.S. Bureau of the Census, Current Housing Reports Series H-150 "Annual Housing Survey" (annual). Latest, 1974--partially available 1974 report contains six parts. 1973 report (first in the series) contains four.

24 U.S. Bureau of the Census, Current Housing Reports Series H-151 "Annual Housing Survey" This report is a supplement to the Series H-150 reports. First H-151 report is for 1973.

25. U.S. Bureau of the Census, Current Housing Reports Series H-170 "Annual Housing Survey: Housing Characteristics for Selected Metropolitan Areas" (annual). A report for 19 selected SMSAs. First reports for 1974 series (first in the series) are partially available.

26. U.S. Bureau of the Census, Current Population Reports Series P-20 No 166 "Households and Families by Type."

27. U.S. Bureau of the Census, Current Population Reports Series P-25 No. 360 "Projections of the Number of Households and Families."

b. Other Federal Government

1. Board of Governors of the Federal Reserve System, Federal Reserve Bulletin (monthly).

2. U.S. Bureau of Domestic Commerce, Construction Review (monthly).

3. U.S. Bureau of Economic Analysis, Fixed Nonresidential Business and Residential Capital in U.S. 1925-75, 1976.

4. U.S. Bureau of Economic Analysis, Survey of Current Business (monthly) (weekly and biennial supplements).

5. U.S. Bureau of Labor Statistics, "Union Wages and Hours: Building Trades" (annual and quarterly).

6. U.S. Bureau of Labor Statistics, "Employment and Earnings" (monthly and annual).

7. U.S. Bureau of Labor Statistics, "Employment and Earnings, States and Areas" (annual).

8. U.S. Bureau of Labor Statistics, "Consumer Price Index" (monthly) (contains housing, rent, and homeownership indices).

9. U.S. Department of Agriculture, Economic Research Service, Farm Real Estate Market Developments (annual with supplements).

10. U.S. Department of Agriculture, Economic Research Service, Farm Real Estate Historical Series Data 1850-1970, 1973.

11. U.S. Department of Housing and Urban Development, The Supply of Mortgage Credit 1970-1974, 1975.

12. U.S. Department of Housing and Urban Development, Annual Report.

13. U.S. Department of Housing and Urban Development, Statistical Yearbook (annual).

14. U.S. Department of Housing and Urban Development "Housing and Urban Development Trends" (monthly and annual). Formerly titled "Housing Statistics."

15. U.S. Department of Housing and Urban Development, FHA Trends (quarterly).

16. U.S. Department of Housing and Urban Development, FHA Homes (annual).

17. U.S. Housing and Home Finance Agency, Housing Statistics, Historical Supplement, October 1961.

18. Federal Home Loan Bank Board, Savings and Home Financing Source Book (annual).

19. Federal Home Loan Bank Board, Annual Report.

20. Federal Home Loan Bank Board, "News" (monthly).

21. The Journal of the Federal Home Loan Bank Board.

22. Annual Report of the Federal Deposit Insurance Corporation.

23. U.S. Department of Health, Education and Welfare, Public Health Service, Vital Statistics of the United States (annual).

24. Veterans Administration, "Loan Guarantee Financial Characteristics" (quarterly).

25. Veterans Administration, "Loan Guarantee Highlights" (monthly).

c. Papers on Data and Other Data Sources

1. Bhatia, K. B. "A Price Index for Nonfarm One-Family Houses, 1947-64" <u>Journal of the American Statistical Association</u>, March 1971, Vol. 66, No. 333, pp. 23-32.

2. Brady, Eugene A. "The Quarterly National Housing Market Data Bank of the Federal Home Loan Bank Board" Federal Home Loan Bank Board Working Paper No. 22, March 1971.

3. Break, George F. <u>The Economic Impact of Federal Loan Insurance</u>, Washington: National Planning Association, 1961.

4. Cassidy, Henry J. "Estimates of the Start-to-Completion Lag for Residential Structures" Federal Home Loan Bank Board Office of Economic Research Working Paper No. 38, October 1972.

5. F. W. Dodge Division, McGraw-Hill Information Systems Co. "Dodge Construction Potentials" (monthly).

6. Freedman, B. N. "Private Housing Completions - A New Dimension in Construction Statistics" Federal Reserve staff paper (abstracted) <u>Federal Residential Bulletin</u>, January 1972, Vol. 58, No. 1, pp. 15-16.

7. Gottlieb, Maunal <u>Long Swings in Urban Development</u>, Urban and Regional Studies No. 4, New York: National Bureau of Economic Research, 1976.

8. Grebler, Leo <u>Housing Issues in Economic Stabilization Policy</u>, Occasional Paper No. 72, New York: National Bureau of Economic Research 1960.

9. Grebler, L., Blank, C. M. and Winnick, L. <u>Capital Formation in Residential Real Estate</u>, Princeton University Press and National Bureau of Economic Research, 1956.

10. Guttentag, Jack M. and Beck, Morris <u>New Series on Home Mortgage Yields Since 1951</u>, National Bureau of Economic Research General Series No 92, London and New York: Columbia University Press for the NBER, 1970.

11. Herzog, John P. and Earley, James S. <u>Home Mortgage Delinquency and Foreclosure</u>, New York: National Bureau of Economic Research, 1970.

12. Klaman, Saul B. <u>The Postwar Residential Mortgage Market</u>, New York: National Bureau of Economic Research, 1961.

13. Lipsey, R. E. and Preston, D.   Source Book of Statistics Relating to Construction, New York: National Bureau of Economic Research, 1966.

14. MacRae, C. Duncan, and Schnare Ann B.   "FHA Activity in Older, Urban, Declining Areas: Options for Evaluation Research" Washington: Urban Institute Contract Report No. 225-5, July 1975.

15. Manvel, Allen   "Trends in the Value of Real Estate and Land, 1956 to 1966" National Commission on Urban Problems Research Report No. 12, Washington, D.C., 1969.

16. Musgrave, J. C.   "New Bureau of the Census Construction Price Indexes"   1968 Proceedings of the Business and Economic Section, American Statistical Association, pp. 374-381.

INDEX OF REFERENCES TO MODELS

National Economic Models

Bosworth-Duesenberry Model (B2):   1, 9, 19, 65-68, 72, 81, 83, 86.

Brookings Model (B3): 5, 7, 9, 14-15, 51, 83.

Bureau of Economic Analysis (BEA) (B4): 1, 5, 7, 11, 14-15, 41,
    45-47, 51, 55, 64, 82.

Chase Econometrics Model (B5): 5, 7, 14-15, 45-46, 58, 82-83.

Data Resources Inc. Model (DRI) (B7):   5, 7, 9, 11, 14-15, 19, 38-39,
    51, 60-61, 64, 66-67, 70, 72, 82-83.

Fair Model (B8): 6-7, 13, 20, 26, 36, 50, 58, 66, 68-69, 82-83.

Hendershott Model (B9): 19, 65, 68, 81, 86.

Hickman-Coen Model (B10): 24, 40, 82.

Liu-Hwa Model (B12): 47, 64.

MIT-Pennsylvania-SSRC Model (MPS) (B13): 1, 5-9, 11-15, 19, 30-31, 33,
    40-48, 51, 54-55, 57, 61-64, 66-68, 71-75, 77-79, 82-83, 86.

Michigan Model (B14): 9, 42, 82, 85, 87.

Silber Model (B15): 4, 19, 51.

Wharton Quarterly Model (B18):   1, 5, 9, 11, 14, 19, 38, 45, 48, 51
    56, 81-83, 85-86.

National Housing Models

Arcelus-Meltzer (C1): 5, 7, 9, 25-26, 49-50.

Brady Model (C2): 5, 7, 20, 25, 47, 49-50, 65, 68-69, 73-74.

Brady Model (C3): 7, 15, 20, 47, 49-50, 73-74, 83.

Cassidy-Valentini Model (C4): 13.

Huang Model (C5): 1, 5, 7, 15, 46, 49, 51, 83.

Huang Model (C6): 20, 46, 47, 49-50, 66, 68, 74-75.

Lin Model (C8): 36, 51-52, 73, 76.

McDonough Model (C9): 16, 18, 36, 51, 64, 83.

Maisel Model (C10): 1, 5, 7, 9, 41, 50, 65, 68, 82.

Muth Model (C11): 5, 11, 13, 41.

Rosen-Kearl Model (C12): 5, 7, 9, 31, 41, 47, 48-51, 60-61, 65-66, 68-69, 77, 82.

Sparks Model (C13): 4, 19, 51, 68, 75.

Swan Model (C14): 5, 65-66.

Swan Model (C15): 5, 9, 13, 26, 30, 38, 49-50, 58-61, 66, 68-69, 83.

Utt Model (C16): 66, 70.

vonFurstenberg-Herr Model (C17): 5, 7, 11, 51, 73, 75.

Other Housing Sector Models

Fair Model (D1): 5, 50.

Huang Model (D2): 16.

Kartman Model (D3): 13, 18, 42, 64.

Krekorian Model (D4): 5, 39, 42.

Pollock Model (D5): 13, 18, 64.

Robins Model (D6): 76-77.

Taubman-Rasche Model (D7): 15, 29, 56.

Winger Model (D8): 5.

Winger Model (D10): 5.

Winger Model (D11): 5.

Related Work

Campbell (F5):   24, 28, 40.

Cargill (F6):   51.

Marcin (F31):   24, 40.

Silber (F40):   31, 65, 69.

Stern (F41):   24, 51.